BRUISED BUT NOT BROKEN

To: Tracy

Not many people can
say they have a
45+ year friendship.
I'm very thankful for
you and our bond.
Love yah.
Caroline
xxx.

Chris Scott Ministries

Chris Scott, Chris Scott Ministries

ISBN 978-1-7360211-6-3 (Paperback)
ISBN 978-1-7360211-5-6 (eBook)

Edited by Christine Bode, Bodacious Copy
Book Cover Design by Trevor Bailey
Book Production by Dawn James, Publish and Promote
Design and Layout by Perseus Design

Printed and bound in the United States of America

Note to the reader: The events in this book are based on the writers' memories from their perspective. Certain names have been changed to protect the identity of those mentioned. The information is provided for educational purposes only. In the event you use any of the information in this book for yourself, which is your constitutional right, the author and publisher assume no responsibility for your actions.

Contents

Introduction

There is no better time than now for these phenomenal women to share part of their life's journey with the world. Rose Dewitt Bukater, in the film *Titanic*, said, "A woman's heart is a deep ocean of secrets." The authors herein released treasures from their hearts to bless you and many others who read these chapters.

When I read these chapters (some on my flight to and from South Africa), the Holy Spirit revealed that the remarkable women of this book are survivors of storms which tried to alter the destiny God has planned for each of them. The title became clear—they are Bruised, but Not Broken. Caroline, CasSandra, Nicola, Brittany, Danielle, Natalie and Tiney are telling their story for God's glory.

God has placed many women with beautiful personalities in my life, and I am eternally grateful. So, let's get a little personal on my relationship with these fabulous women as I address the following few lines of this introduction to each of them.

Minister CasSandra, the day I walked into your class, your un-matched beauty and no-nonsense leadership let me know that you were about your Father's (God) business. I thank you for what you poured into me almost ten years ago. You are such a beautiful soul. I am grateful to be part of your journey. Your strength for life's storms is evident in the glow you transmit in a room. I love you.

Natalie, my love. I thank God for allowing me the opportunity to share beautiful memories with you. I often look back on that perfect sunlit day in May as I helped guide your horse and car-riage down the path to join your king as he anxiously awaited his queen on a plush, perfectly manicured lawn. Your vivacious smile that day will permanently be etched in my mind. I love you.

Nicola, I am proud of you. I watched you work long hours to provide for your children. I witnessed you walking to get to work many days when you did not have a vehicle. You were a mother on a mission to ensure you kept food on the table and shoes on your children's feet. The anointing in your life and answering "the Call" to Ministry leads me to believe that God is pleased. You always (truly) had the most radiant smile on your face, no matter what trials came your way. I love you.

My baby doll Brittany, I thank God for placing you in my life to love. You are such a delicate rose with a heart of gold. The day I witnessed your precious daddy walk you down the aisle to meet your Kareem, I stood as a surrogate mother with tears in my eyes, thanking God for saving your life. My most vivid memory of the love you and my dear brother Garth shared was the day I saw you both in the doctor's office on your journey to healing. He was al-ways by your side as he is now. I love you. You are a treasure.

"Queen Daughter" as you are in my life. Thank you for being as beautiful as you are. God sent you to cover me in prayer, and for this, I am grateful. You are indeed a treasure to the Kingdom of God, and I love how you use your gifts and talents to enhance the lives of those you meet. I have seen some of your challenges with your move from Detroit to Atlanta, but God kept you. There were times you almost let go and returned, but your strength always kicked in. See you on the big screen again. I love you.

My dearest Caroline, the first time we met, your smile lit up the room with joy and confidence, enhancing your beautiful and exuberant personality. Your Caribbean heritage, coupled with your British upbringing, is a fusion that provides a passion that shines as a bright light in a dark room. Your life reminds me of this famous quote by Dr. Martin Luther King, "Darkness cannot drive out darkness; only light can do that. Hate cannot drive out hate; only love can do that". So continue to "Be Love." I love you.

Dr. Tiney Ray, I shall never forget the excitement in your voice when we first spoke. I remember exactly where I was when you called because you made my spirit leap with joy. At that moment, I realized you had a passion and mandate to change women's lives everywhere. The blessing further manifested in hearing your story of being a teenage mom, which was similar to my journey. We faced rejection and were almost exiled, but God! Thank you for your love and friendship, Coach. I love you.

We often endure betrayal, negativity, and fear, yet we are "Bruised but Not Broken." For the women in this book, I leave you with my favorite poem by Dr. Maya Angelou to walk in whom God has called you to be. Make no apologies for being the Phenomenal Woman you are.

Phenomenal Woman
BY MAYA ANGELOU

Pretty women wonder where my secret lies.
I'm not cute or built to suit a fashion model's size
But when I start to tell them,
They think I'm telling lies.
I say,
It's in the reach of my arms,
The span of my hips,
The stride of my step
The curl of my lips.
I'm a woman
Phenomenally.
Phenomenal woman,
That's me.

I walk into a room
Just as cool as you please,
And to a man,
The fellows stand or
Fall down on their knees.
Then they swarm around me,
A hive of honey bees.
I say,
It's the fire in my eyes,
And the flash of my teeth,
The swing in my waist,
And the joy in my feet.
I'm a woman
Phenomenally.

Phenomenal woman,
That's me.

Men themselves have wondered
What they see in me.
They try so much
But they can't touch
My inner mystery.
When I try to show them,
They say they still can't see.
I say,
It's in the arch of my back,
The sun of my smile,
The ride of my breasts,
The grace of my style.
I'm a woman
Phenomenally.
Phenomenal woman,
That's me.

Now you understand
Just why my head's not bowed.
I don't shout or jump about
Or have to talk real loud.
When you see me passing,
It ought to make you proud.
I say,
It's in the click of my heels,
The bend of my hair,
The palm of my hand,
The need for my care.
'Cause I'm a woman

Phenomenally.
Phenomenal woman,
That's me.

CHAPTER 1

Getting through Hills and Valleys

by Natalie Raines

Have you ever thought about what your purpose in life may be? Why you may be going through the things that you are experiencing? Then, you look at how life appears to be going for other people and compare yours with theirs.

Well, you are not the only one. Finding your life's purpose can be very hard to figure out. When you think you have it all figured out, something changes the direction of your course. Then you are back to a starting position, but the starting position has changed. Life is an evolution of cycles. We will go through many trials and tribulations, but how long you remain in the valley of self-doubt is up to you.

August of 1996 was my freshman year at the University of Louisville, and I started engineering school. I was determined to be the first person in my family to graduate college. I didn't realize this was the most pivotal moment in my life. Growing up, there were difficult and painful times, but this was the first time I didn't have my parents to help guide me. I was now a woman and had to figure things out. I was always headstrong and proud and didn't like asking for help. In my mind, I was going to figure it out myself. Engineering school was extremely mentally tough on me. I felt like giving up many times and throwing my books at the walls because I was so frustrated. I hated school for the first time in my life. I saw my friends who didn't have classes as challenging get to go out more and genuinely enjoy college.

On the other hand, I was resentful and wanted to give up. But, at the same time of wanting to give up and just throw in the towel; I didn't want to hurt my parents. I had strong expectations of making my parents proud, but I struggled badly.

I remember sitting in church one Sunday morning as a freshman in college. I was going through some really challenging things at school. I remember the pastor talking about hills and valleys. Life was never designed for us to live a flat life. Instead, God created it so that we will experience both hills and valleys. The hills in life are when everything is going well. We are at the top during that season, and we assume that since we are at the highest peak, we will always remain in that position. But there is no way we can always stay at the peak, and we must endure the valleys of life.

During the valleys in life, we go through the trenches. Things are not going well, and it seems we will always remain in the valley and never see the light of our situation. The pastor said it was up to the individual how long they would stay in the valley. If they didn't put faith in God that He would lead them on the right path through the valley, they would always remain in it.

After leaving the church that Sunday, I had a lot on my mind. I was mad and resentful that the path that I had been shown to becoming an engineer was so challenging. I questioned why I couldn't be like my friends and enjoy their college experience. I was so tired of always crying and constantly failing. I wasn't used to failing in school. If anything, school always came easy to me, and I had so many terrific experiences in high school that no other kids ever got to experience. I was at the peak of the mountain in high school. I was an honor student and was chosen to be part of many leadership programs that took me to Germany and Andover, MA, every summer. Only a select few were ever asked to experience these things, especially a young Black female. So having challenges in college made me resentful. I didn't realize then that I was going through my first valley as a woman.

I remember calling my mom crying and telling her that I was quitting engineering school and going to Boston College. She calmed me down and said to try engineering school for one year. If I was still struggling after that year, then to look at changing directions. She challenged me to put my all into my studies and change my attitude toward engineering school.

I remembered that sermon in which the pastor discussed hills and valleys. I prayed for God to give me the strength to make it through and that I needed Him to make it. This was the turning point in my college career. I had to change how I looked at the situation. I knew I would never make it if I kept fighting through it alone. So, I prayed for God to give me peace and balance. I asked my friends to help me keep a schedule. I would study during certain times, but if they saw that I was becoming too stressed to pull me outside and go have some fun.

God sent me one of my best friends during this time. We were the only Black females in the class, and we hated it. So, we started to study together and then became inseparable. Becoming friends with her at that time in my life helped me through that valley as we helped each other.

Long story short, I graduated from the University of Louisville with a bachelor's and Master's of Industrial Engineering. God put me in a leadership position as the President of NSBE (National Society of Black Engineers). I helped inspire many Black students to hang in and stick it out. That together we could make it. During my tenure as president, we had the largest number of Black students graduate from engineering. I always credited that sermon with helping to change my attitude toward life and my intense love for coaching and mentoring.

After graduating with my Master of Industrial Engineering with a 3.8 GPA, I felt like I was on cloud nine. I accepted an offer with a Fortune 500 company as a line supervisor. So, there I was at the top of the hill again, but I didn't realize I would start descending to the valley fast. I was one of the youngest and the only Black female supervisor in that company. I was about twenty-four; the average employee was a forty-eight-year-old white male. Lord knew this was going to be one rocky road.

At first, my employees didn't respect me for being younger or the age of their children. Anything that I asked them to do was responded with very harsh and hateful comments. I had grown men yelling and cursing in my face; all I can remember was the hate in their eyes. This was not the first time that racism presented itself in my life, but this was the first outright racism and sexism as a woman. The building was an old state prison, and I felt like I was in prison daily.

That job kept me isolated by continuously rotating my shifts, so I didn't get to see my family as much and for sure didn't have time for church. I had to work every Sunday at 10:00 p.m., so I slept most of the day. I became depressed and felt isolated from the world. I felt like God had completely left me. I had entirely left the church because I had a massive falling out with the pastor. He had totally disrespected me and then stated that God led him to do that to make an example of me in front of the church. I told him that any God that said that to him was not my God, so I left. Then I began to go deeper and deeper into the valley. The trail was dark and lonely, with no trace of ever getting out.

At twenty-four years old, I injured my hip and couldn't walk for over a year. Even after having hip repair surgery, I couldn't walk without a crutch or a wheelchair. I remember thinking, *GOD, WHY ME?!* Money was running short because, during this time, I couldn't work. I cried most nights for God to send me a signal. The night before I went from short-term disability to long-term disability, I stayed up all night crying. How was I going to pay my bills? Finally, at 7:00 a.m., I received a phone call from one of my maintenance workers. He stated that God told him to call me and to follow everything he was about to tell me. And within the next day, I would have my job back and return to work that week. God answered my prayers, so I got up and did exactly what he told me to do. Within twenty-four hours, my job called and told me they were making provisions for me to return to work that Wednesday. That was nothing but God, as He had heard my cry, and I knew then that I had to get back into the church.

The following Sunday, I found my new church home, and low and behold, my parents and half of my family were at that same service. God told me He had a plan for me, but I had to listen to what He said. So, I returned to work for that company, and within a year, God revealed His next plan for me. He had found a job for me in Atlanta, GA, and it was the job of my dreams. I had left wandering the valley for four years to finally be on top of the hill. ATL, here I come! But I had never thought I would leave my family behind and move to another state.

Moving to Atlanta was another chapter in my life. In the beginning, I was lonely and depressed that I had moved so far away from my family. Thoughts of quitting were almost daily, but I truly loved what I was doing. A year after I moved to Atlanta, God sent my brother to live with me. No longer was I alone, and I knew my brother would have my back if I needed him. So, I started to settle into life in the ATL. I continued to thrive within my company and build a brand for myself. And, low and behold, God sent me my amazing husband. I wasn't looking for him, but it was time that I found someone who truly loved me. Someone who could help us both become better people. We are complete opposites, but I felt this God-fearing man was right for me. May 2011 was one of the best days of my life. I married my best friend.

Within one year of marriage, I faced a forever-changing thing. My older sister passed away from cancer. That event was the most challenging thing I had endured. I remember being the first person to go to hospice and see that sign on the door that the person there had died. The day before her passing, the family was there to help support her. Her personality shined through all the way to the end.

The month after my sister passed, I discovered I was pregnant with my first daughter. This was a shock as doctors had previously told me I would never have children. When my family found out it was a girl, all thoughts went to my sister. God had gained an angel but sent us an angel too. This really helped us through our grieving process.

When my daughter was born, she had many health issues and was in and out of the hospital every six weeks because of her breathing. Her hair began to fall out, and she couldn't hold down her formula for months. Having a sickly baby was when I realized I was going through, yet again, another valley. My husband and I took her to all the best doctors, but none of them could help identify why she was always sick. The final straw was when I was pregnant with my second daughter, and my oldest was rushed to the hospital, where she almost coded. LORD, why are you taking this little baby through this?

Seeing my baby in the ICU for a week made me an emotional wreck, and I felt hopeless. I felt like I couldn't help my baby, and the doctors were using her as a pin cushion and not trying to heal her. So, I went into solid prayer. *God, please heal my baby.* I remember when God told me to fire all her doctors, and He would heal her. So, I fired all the doctors, and God provided two Naturopathic doctors, each focusing on different areas. He also led me to start studying to become a holistic coach. Within ninety days, my baby girl was healed as I followed the path. *Thank you, God,* for saving my baby girl.

While healing my daughter, I can genuinely say that this was the first time I followed His every word. I was starting to grow spiritually and finally learning God's voice. I tell everyone that through listening to God, my baby was healed. If I had not listened to Him, there is no telling what would have happened to my daughter.

When trouble comes my way, I always go back to that sermon in 1996. I will not always stay in the valley but listening and following His voice will lead me back to the top of the mountain. See, what I was starting to learn about as I matured in my spirituality was that I was never in control of my life. It was God leading my way, and all I had to do was listen for His voice.

The year 2020 was the year that my faith was truly tested. I started a new job in January as God led me to leave the company I'd worked at for fifteen years to do something different. This role offered the salary I had been praying for. Finally, we were no longer living paycheck to paycheck, but the position I took on was a traveling job which meant I was away from the family Monday through Thursday. I knew that I needed to make a sacrifice for my family and that I couldn't do this for a long time.

March 2020 is when the world shut down. First, the company I worked for started talking about furlough, and I knew deep down that it would affect me. Then, in April 2020, it was announced that in May 2020, I would be 100 percent furloughed through the summer. This meant that I would be on unemployment benefits while on furlough.

My friend started selling clothes out of her closet on Facebook, which was taking off like wildfire. She had asked me to start selling my clothes on her page, but the fear of going live was too much for me. Plus, I had lost over 130 pounds and had donated most of my clothes, so I didn't have enough clothes to go live. Another friend started going live on her Facebook page and begged me to sell. But again, I thought I didn't have enough clothes. Then, one day as I was cleaning out bins underneath my bed, I found 200 pieces of vintage clothing. This was God's way of telling me to start selling. April 29, 2020, was my first Livestream; I didn't know that my job would call five days later to inform me that I was being laid off.

I remember breaking down in the shower. Cried my heart out because I was unsure how I would provide for my family, although our household was a two-income household. When I say I cried, I cried my heart out. Praying and asking God for direction because I couldn't believe that I no longer had an income. God allowed me twenty-four hours to mourn the loss of my job. The next day He stated, *I already prepared you for this. Remember those clothes you found underneath your bed, and you started doing Livestreams?* He said *this is how you will be able to provide for your family.*

At the time, we lived in a small three-bedroom house, and with everyone stuck in the place due to COVID-19, I took a small part of my girls' playroom to store my clothes. I went hard on live streaming and then started exploring lives on other platforms; some weeks, I did three to four lives a week. People saw my smile on camera, but nobody saw that I would show up every Tuesday for a food giveaway to help feed the family while continuing to build my business.

While I was doing lives, I was also looking for jobs. My old company had paid for a company that helped with my resume and provided tips for finding a job. I would attend these group meetings every week, but it was depressing to continue attending. At that time, so many were laid off, and it was hard to find a job. God told me to stop attending the calls as He had me. He told me when it was time for me to get a job, it would come. So, I continued to push through with lives the entire summer. God continued to provide for my family, and we continued to be blessed.

Then out of the blue, I got a call from a recruiter stating that he found my resume on LinkedIn and thought I was the perfect person for an IT Project Management Temp role. The pay was about the same as I was making before being laid off. I did one interview and was told they loved me and offered me the temp role, which would be 100 percent home-based. God told me to take the job and focus on my business. So, in the midst of working and building my business, I continued to listen to everything He told me to do. Yes, most of what He told me to do was uncomfortable, but I persisted.

I remember being asked by a family member to be a spokesperson for her Zoom group called "When life gives you lemons, you make lemonade!" I was so shocked that I was being asked to speak. She stated that she had been watching my testimony and that it was time to share it with others. The fact that I lost my job but never gave up faith that God would continue to be there with me. She said you inspire so many people, and you have no clue that you encourage them to never give up. During my speech, I told the attendees I would not be here if it weren't for God and that if I didn't listen to His word, there is no telling where my family would be. It is because of God that I am here. Yes, there were times when I wanted to give up, but I had to lean on Him.

2020 had so many hills and valleys and was such an emotional roller coaster. Who would have ever thought that when losing my job at the beginning of the year, all bills would be paid, and my family would never go hungry for one day? It was nothing but God!! In October 2020, I remember my husband stating that we should look for houses because our house was too small. I told him he was out of his mind and we couldn't afford that. I didn't realize that God was setting us up for another chapter. I doubted that we could do it, but it was my husband's faithfulness and listening to God. Never in my wildest dreams would I think the next miracles would ever happen.

In a very short time, we became credit card and loan free except for the mortgage. And on December 20, 2020, we moved into our dream home. Now you can't tell me that it was nothing but the Lord that made that happen. Debt-free with a new home after losing my job only six months earlier. My mom told me that because I told people that God was taking the lead and I just followed, my family was awarded the new home.

Throughout my life, I have endured so many hills and valleys. Sometimes I wanted to give up, but God never allowed me to. I have learned that your attitude on life will be the direction of how your life goes down. Life is made up of choices. You can choose to have an attitude of doing the right thing or the wrong thing. However, if you make the wrong choice, you must remember that you can always hit the Reset button. Hitting the Reset button is repenting to God that you made a bad choice. He is a forgiving God, but you must listen to Him about what direction you have to take.

As I continue building up my family and business, God has brought many terrific people into my life and has been preparing me to coach and mentor. I never started on this journey to inspire people but mainly to help my family. But God stated *you must help others. They are watching you and how you maneuver.* Sometimes I feel like I am not good enough and wonder why these people are reaching out to me. I am just a woman who is living. But God reminds me that I am never alone and that He is using me to help deliver others. My imperfections are part of God's plan to make my life the plan He designed for me.

I am forever grateful for having such a fantastic husband who holds me and reminds me that God will not leave me. When I cry about an outcome that doesn't go to my plan, my husband reminds me that God still has us. Our family is in His favor, and I must remember that. Before each Livestream, my husband tells me to pray that the outcome will be what God wants it to be. I notice a huge difference in my lives if I don't pray before. I feel out of order.

This is my testimony that God never left me. First, I must remember who the woman is behind the photo and camera. My life's testimony is that there will be hills and valleys, but when life gives you lemons, make lemonade. Lemons are very tart, but we make lemonade by adding a little sugar. Lemonade is refreshing and sweet. Sometimes when things go wrong, it is how you look at the situation that will make a change and press the Reset button. And that change is part of God's plan for your life. Just believe and follow His word. Remember that the way that your relationship with God and how God speaks to each person is very personal. He knows your heart and can tell when you are grateful for what He has done for you. There will be many more hills and valleys in life, but I know through the grace of God, He will make sure we make it through.

ABOUT THE AUTHOR

Natalie Raines was born and raised in Louisville, Kentucky. Natalie has a Master's of Industrial Engineering, is a certified Holistic Coach, a Certified Life Coach, and is the CEO of Naturally Natalie and Kollections by Natalie. Her faith and family are the most important factors in her life. She enjoys spending time with her friends and family in her spare time.

www.NatalieRaines.info
www.kollectionsbynatalie.shop
www.facebook.com/kollectionsbynatalie
www.facebook.com/groups/fashionistatribe
www.instagram.com/kollectionsbynatalie/

CHAPTER 2

Spices in My Caravan

by Nicola C. Darlington

The story of my life is summarized in one sentence: when your enemies or life, in general, puts you in a caravan, God makes sure it is preloaded with supplies to ensure you make it to the other end. To be exact, He makes sure that spices, balm and myrrh are in it before you even start your journey. But, unfortunately, most of us don't make it whole to the other end because we are so fixated on the caravan itself that we lose focus of the provisions already placed in it before we were co-opted in.

I know this is not how a chapter of my personal life is supposed to begin. Protocol and tradition cause most of us to start with the usual niceties of when and where we were born, what elementary and advanced schools we went to and occasionally, good friends we lost along the way. And then, after that, we sag into the moment when tragedy hit us and then to the good part about how we made it despite the odds stacked against us.

In this chapter, I chose to dispense with tradition but concentrate instead on the spices God put in the caravan that took me from the land of innocence, peace and harmony I knew to strange emotional and traumatic physical landscapes that altered my life forever.

Let me talk about the caravan first so you know where I am coming from. In the Bible, in the Book of Genesis, there is a young man named Joseph. He was a dreamer and interpreter of dreams who was so loved by his father, Jacob. He had a dream that he shared with his father and brothers. In the dream, his father and brothers were bowing down before him. He shared it with his brothers, who hated him for it and looked for an opportunity to get rid of him. Talk about sharing your dream with the wrong people.

One day his father sent him to check on his brothers and deliver much-needed food supplies. They saw him from afar, said, "Here comes the dreamer," and decided to kill him. One brother had enough sense to convince the other brothers to throw him in a pit instead. And then, another came up with the idea of selling him to some merchants passing by. These merchants had a caravan preloaded with spices, balm and myrrh.

The Bible could have talked about the people already in the caravan or other essential supplies like water and honey, but special mention is given to these spices. They gained prominence in his story because they represent people and events that orchestrated his deliverance from his traumatic experience at such a tender age.

I grew up in a loving home. Daddy and mommy loved me a lot, and unlike Joseph, I had a great relationship with my brother and sisters. I was dad's girl and even have his nose and some of his character attributes. He was a great provider, and Mom was the best homemaker you could ask for. But the love surrounding me in my home could not shelter me from the horrific caravan experience I found myself in.

Let me define a typical caravan experience so you can better understand the gravity of what happened to me and shaped me into the person I am. A caravan experience is an unexpected event that happens to an innocent person without prior warning. And from the moment it hits you, your life is altered permanently, and it is never the same again. It may take an entire lifetime for you to fully recover from its effects, and you will always carry the scars in your body and soul, permanently reminding you that you were dealt a horrible card at the most crucial time of your development as a human being.

Mine happened to me on the most perfect Kingston, Jamaica evening. Reggae music was in the air, and somewhere on the island, I am sure hummingbirds were getting ready to retire after a long day of sucking nectar out of beautiful flowers. The torrential rain that fell upon me on that dreadful night was not preceded by dark clouds hanging above nor by an advance warning from the weather forecast team. There was no lingering foul odor in the atmosphere to warn me something was about to hit me so hard that my life would never be the same again. I am sure if Joseph was to tell his story, it would sound the same. Sent by his dad to check on his brothers and replenish their food supplies, he didn't know that a plot, a pit and a caravan were waiting for him.

And when it comes to narrating this part of my story, I prefer to do so in the voice of the little girl in me who was violated in the most brutal way imaginable. She waited a long time to tell her story, but now this is her opportunity. She will tell you why she continued to cry on the inside of me even though I was now a grown woman and mother. You will understand why she was a late bloomer and why it took so many years for her bubbly life and infectious smile to come out. And for those in a similar situation, I want you to understand that until that little grieving girl/boy on the inside of you is healed, you will continue to cry unprovoked tears and suffer pain that no doctor or therapist can document on a piece of paper.

I was a huge sports fan, especially soccer and netball, and I never missed a game unless something was really wrong. Maybe it was the thrill of watching twenty-two young men chasing and kicking an inflated round ball back and forth, never getting tired for ninety minutes, and scoring only one goal after all that effort. They rarely scored more than two goals in a game. Netball was the same, except they kept the ball up in the air until someone threw it through a net. Soccer was fascinating because, unlike American football, which is played by bulky men, sometimes 350 pounds, all it requires is your skill, and some of the greatest soccer players weighed less than 130 pounds. In football, only one person is allowed to kick the ball—the rest must use their hands. In soccer, only one person can use his hands—the rest must use their feet! I loved sports and paid the ultimate price on its field.

One evening after coming from a function where a group of us went to represent our school, I walked across the soccer field where our team played. It was dark but nothing to be scared about because it was the same road I always took home. It was a typical soccer field, bumpy and dusty, surrounded by houses of varying styles and sizes, not subject to any HOA regulations. Halfway through the field, three men appeared out of nowhere, grabbed me and dragged me to the side of the soccer field where there were a few bushes. I remember hitting the ground hard. Then I was ordered to take off my clothes, and when I took my time to comply, they took matters into their own hands. They started to rape me one after another for a good forty-five minutes. Mercilessly they violated my body like piranhas devouring a carcass in murky waters, only they took turns and passed me from one man to another like I was a soccer ball. I took every painful thrust and tear of my flesh with my mouth muffled like a sheep to the slaughter. Finally, in my pain, I mastered enough strength to talk to God and asked Him just to let me live, and He heard me.

And just like that, my virginity and innocence were taken away from me in the most violent and painful manner imaginable. This is not how I envisioned my first encounter with a man, but again it's a caravan experience that we are talking about. I had kept my virginity out of self-pride, not because of religious reasons or stern orders from my parents. It was my badge of differentiation from the other girls around me, and I wanted to be different.

In typical caravan experience fashion, a subsequent visit to the doctor resulted in the worst news ever: I would not be able to conceive and have children because my uterus had been badly damaged from the ordeal. In a span of forty-five minutes, the thing I had treasured my whole life was taken away from me, and all I was left with was bloody underwear, throbbing pain all over my lower body and a damaged uterus. I picked myself up and stumbled back to the path to go home. I was so traumatized I couldn't remember for over thirty years what I did between those bushes and my house until a few weeks ago when I started writing my story. What I am about to tell you now is information that was frozen in me for years, and my brain kept it for me and not from me until now.

I say for me because had I known then what I know now, I would have killed myself out of shame. But, instead, I now know that I staggered home and, on my way, I told everybody I met my story. I told total strangers I had been violently raped and asked them why as if they knew the answer. I finally made it home and told my parents and siblings, and they all cried with me.

The adults retraced my footsteps to the neighborhood and asked around for the names of the culprits, but they all professed their ignorance. This was Jamaica—snitches get stitches. And with no closure, the fate of this little girl was sealed, and I was firmly in my caravan.

I grieved the loss of my virginity and endured the pain and permanent scarring inflicted upon my body. Every day I asked why me, of all the girls and women who frequented the same road through that soccer field. I wondered silently if I did anything to provoke them to attack me like that. And then I found an easy way out—blame it on my body shape and beauty. I reasoned that maybe if I wasn't as rounded as I am, they would not have targeted me. So, from that time, I started to hate my body and blame myself for everything that went wrong in my life.

And then, I started to question my ability to make sound decisions. To me, it was simple logic; I made the wrong decision to use that cut-through road. As a result, I couldn't trust myself to make sound decisions.

And then another thought came to me, and I accommodated it. Maybe it was the young men whose advances I had rejected or other jealous young girls I hung with who spitefully connived with my rapists. Was it coincidental that I was walking alone and none of my friends were there with me? I, therefore, made another life-altering decision; don't trust anyone or allow them to get too close to you. Just like that, I shut myself off from a lot of people and internalized my feelings and pain, and up to this day, it takes a lot for me to trust anyone. And you only have one chance to mess it up, and that's the end of it.

My life's journey as a broken girl and woman started that dreadful day. And broken women usually attract broken men: it's just the way it is. I dated losers and lost a lot along the way. But one thing I didn't lose is my self-confidence, and I sure know who I am. I can assure you right now that it will not happen again if I have something to say about it.

I have rebuilt myself from the inside out, and let me tell you something. The house they sought to destroy has been made over into a mansion. Remember the spices I talked about at the beginning of my story? They are in every caravan that anyone finds themselves in. I tapped into them and transitioned into the beautiful, successful, trendsetting gifted woman and proud mother of three that you see today. If there is anything that I learned from this whole experience and process of becoming whole again, it is to embrace the spices and not concentrate on the caravan itself.

The caravan is scary, and sometimes it takes you where angels tread but always remember that it also carries spices to restore you and take you places you never imagined.

The three spices that I am talking about are spices proper, balm and myrrh. These are the same spices Joseph embraced and received his restoration from a slave to a governor. Talk about a comeback!

My favorite is myrrh. It is a fragrant gum resin which mainly comes from a small bushy tree cultivated in the Arabian Peninsula. The grower makes a small cut in the bark, where the gum resin leaks out. It is then collected and stored for about three months until it hardens into fragrant globules. Myrrh is used raw or crushed and mixed with oil to make perfume. It is also used medicinally to reduce swelling and stop pain. But, most importantly, it is a preservative which is why Joseph of Arimathea and Nicodemus brought a mixture of seventy-five pounds of myrrh and aloes to anoint Jesus's body, then wrapped it in linen cloths and laid it in the tomb.

Please note that it only comes out after you make a small cut in the bark. It is available to anyone anytime life bruises you or you are cut deep into your soul. Until you are cut, you don't know it is available for the taking. In an allegorical sense, myrrh is the survival instinct that kicks in when life deals you an unfair card and inner strength, gifts, and abilities that you never knew you had that suddenly manifest. It could also be a gift or talent you knew you had, but it is amplified a million times when you go through your caravan experience.

Myrrh is the inner strength that a divorced woman finds to go back to college and get a PhD when a university degree was the furthest thing from her mind when everything was going right. It is the inexplicable spirit of entrepreneurship and creativity that suddenly grips a person who was wrongfully terminated to come up with the most remarkable invention or product for a niche market that no one has seen before. You know when it oozes out of you because you will always say I never knew I could…or I never knew I was capable of such and such.

My myrrh was the sudden brilliance and maturity that I got. I just knew things from that day forward, and even today, I just know what's up. I sense the pain hidden deep inside a person, and I just know what someone is going through. Something awoke inside me that day and has been my sustaining gift ever since.

Another myrrh for me was the spirit of discernment. Maybe my spirit picked up on something in that dingy place where they violated me that it instantly recognizes it and its cousins whenever they show up. In seconds I sense negative energy in the environment whenever it shows up. My dreams are also very exact, and I usually see in visions what is to come or is about to happen long before it manifests.

Academically I started to perform better than I did before the incident. A sudden burst of intelligence just fell upon me, and what was difficult before was suddenly easy peasy now. Where was this gift before I was cut really deep? Doors started to open for me, culminating in my admission to one of Jamaica's prestigious teacher training colleges. To this day, wherever I go, power brokers, movers and shakers are drawn to my personality and intellect and trust me with their secrets. Isn't it amazing what myrrh can do after you have been cut?

Then there are spices proper. Spices elevate you and your persona just like they turn blunt food into something delectable. They interrupt the rhythm of an otherwise directionless life that seemingly is going nowhere and give it the swag and surf it deserves.

They usually come in the form of specially sent people and moments that "spice up" your life in the midst of what you going through. And when most people encounter them, they say it was a lucky encounter, but I disagree. To me, luck is when God shows up in your situation or circumstances without announcing His name or presence. They are the momentous occasions out of nowhere that come to tickle you and pick you up from your self-pity. Remember those unsolicited hugs of an innocent child when you felt unwanted and rejected? And words of affirmation from a total stranger at a traffic light when someone rolled down their window and told you how much God loves you? Yeah, that's them showing up just in the nick of time.

I have met some really nice people in my life, which restored my faith in the goodness of humanity. On the other hand, I ran the risk of hating people, especially men, after my experience. I understand why some women never want to be bothered with men and go the other way with their sexuality or just opt to remain single. Bad apples not only spoil the bunch but ruin a farmer's life.

Authentic, genuinely nice people are all around us. We just need to discern them and not fall for the Ishmaels who come before Jacob. But, most importantly, I am persuaded that somewhere up there and here on earth, there is God who really cares for His people and turns the bad that befalls them into good, happy-ending stories.

Like Joseph, my spices have come mainly from people—the right people—who have shown up at the right time. In Joseph's case, strangers in Egypt affirmed him and elevated him to be the ruler of the house Potiphar despite his continued status as a slave. And then, when he went to prison or his second pit, the humor of God amid a hopeless situation manifested again. He was elevated to be overseer of the prison and placed in the same quarters with former high-ranking officials who used to serve Pharoah on a daily basis. I mean, what are the odds?

In my imagination, I hear them reminiscing how Pharoah totally made a fool of himself one day when he drank too much wine from the hands of the cupbearer. I believe that he learned the ways of Pharaoh from these two high-ranking officials who had served him up close. It was a setup for his next position as Pharoah's deputy with inside information gathered from fellow prisoners. This is what I call a setup for greatness.

But his most prominent spice to me was the day he saw his little brother Benjamin whom he had left back home without the usual byes when he was sold to the Ishmaelites by his jealous brothers. I don't know what kind of day he was having that day, but whatever it was, it shifted the moment he saw his little brother. Lingering questions he had were answered in that one moment. Did they also sell him like they did me after I left? No wonder why he cried tears of joy.

And then his brothers who sold him bowed down to him thinking they were bowing to some Egyptian ruler—for food. The very thing they sold him for is what they did in fulfillment of his dream. Spices don't get more aromatic than that!

So, what were my spices? I will put my three girls at the top of that culinary list. Remember, the doctor told me I could not have children. I got not just one but three to prove that many are the plans and utterances of men, but it is the purpose of the Lord that prevails. Three spices, each with its own distinct aroma.

Nikala is the cooling spice that gives the mouth a refreshing taste, like sweet mint or sweet basil. Her uncanny demeanor causes everything around our home to reset and find the perfect rhythm. She is the most refreshing person I know to be around. Cool as a cucumber and untroubled by heat or exertion.

Then there is Amanda, the fruity spice which tastes exactly how you expect it to. She is the most consistent and colorful person I know. She is so grounded and accomplishes whatever she puts her mind to. If she sees food she likes, Amanda will research the recipe and try it until she gets it right. She is still in high school, but she already has a successful hair-braiding business of her own.

Lastly, Abbie—the floral spice. That girl right there is as colorful as they come and brightens every room she walks into. She is sophisticated and elegant, and surprisingly strong. She can be peppery at times but still share aromatic qualities that trigger the smell receptors that line your nose and throat. She turns an average outfit into a designer piece with just one simple twist.

Our best moments together are when we all hang loose and put on some reggae music and just dance. In a sense, they help me to relieve my youthful years that were unceremoniously interrupted at the hands of three diabolic men. It also doesn't hurt to let them know I still got it.

I found myself down on my face after my divorce in Atlanta, and my life almost reverted to the old pattern where I had high highs and really low lows. I could have become homeless, but for my brother-in-law and sister who took us in. They have become second parents to my girls, a favor I have also returned to their kids. I can always count on them on any dark day to spice things up and get me going.

During this time, when my life became unsteady and unbearable, another spice was sent by God to reset my life, and it was none other than the owners of Select Meats and Produce. And when I needed to go to the next level in my walk with God, He sent me many wonderful men and women of God to guide and teach me the word of God from the Hebraic perspective. Over time, they have created an environment where I have blossomed to become a respectable woman of God, free to exercise the gifts and talents that God gave me.

I have so many spices to thank God for that I can't list them all. My high school teacher, who hooked me up with a group of nuns who used to visit Jamaica for their annual conference, stands out of the bunch. That relationship led me to my first position as a teacher at a Catholic prep school. The girl scouts movement exposed me to the USA via the student exchange program, where I met some wonderful families in the Midwest.

I can truly say that I am colorful, sweet and vivacious, thanks to the spices in my caravan.

I saved the best for the last—balm. Balm is a fragrant ointment or preparation used to heal or soothe the skin. There are many references to balm in the Bible, especially the one from Gilead.

So you can get the myrrh, which stands for the gifts and inspiration you get after life has bruised you, and spices which represent the people and moments that show up at the right moment to lift you, but you still need healing. Pain is not a respecter of people; it affects the rich and the poor, the common and the famous alike, and one thing we all need is healing.

Let me address pain (physical, emotional and spiritual) first. All pain has an expiration date. You just have to enforce that date. Most of us still carry pain that should have been discarded long ago. The Bible says, "Weeping may endure for a night, but joy comes in the morning." In other words, there is a set period for weeping, and every created soul is promised joy in the morning. Weeping that spills into your mourning has overstepped its boundaries.

I can be vulnerable now despite what happened to me because I am healed. I am healed physically, emotionally and spiritually. We are made of these three parts: the body, soul and spirit and whatever affects one of these entities impacts the others.

I received my physical healing, as evidenced by my three daughters. That healing happened behind the scenes and restored my physical body, but emotional healing was not so easy. I had to go through a grueling process that was preceded by acquiring appropriate knowledge and understanding.

I had to understand, first and foremost, that emotional healing cannot take place outside the grieving process. Grief is the process that enables you to acknowledge your pain and the loss you suffered and face it head-on. You can't be healed from something you have not acknowledged or are numbing through other coping mechanisms. You got to mourn your loss until you are cleansed from it. God did it after the first couple sinned against him, and their offspring started to sin big time. Genesis 6, verses 5 and 6, says, "Then the LORD saw that the wickedness of man was great upon the earth and that every inclination of the thoughts of his heart was altogether evil all the time. And the LORD regretted that He had made man on the earth, and He was grieved in His heart."

God counted His loss and was grieved in His heart. God grieved and then came up with a plan. We spiritualize too much and label people who are still getting their healing as not saved enough. Healing is an act and a process; you just have to embrace the process.

I started by writing down the loss that I suffered and the pain that I experienced. I gave myself the liberty to describe it in the most graphic terms I could think of. Luckily enough, it was not posted to anyone. And since I have not had the opportunity to meet the vile men who raped me, I wrote anonymous letters to each of them, expressing how disgusted I was with them. I let them know that only cowardly men violate a woman the way they did me. And to take turns on me was the most animalistic behavior I had ever witnessed in my entire life. So you go ahead and guess where I wished they spent the rest of their lives if they did not repent of their diabolic sin. I am being honest, but I cursed them and told them a thing or two about whoever raised them.

And then I took those letters, built the most enormous fire ever, and burned them one by one. I took the ashes, put them in a dirty plastic bag, and threw them into a dustbin. I made sure the garbage people collected it because that one needed to go.

Maybe I have watched too many Iyanla Vanzant *Fix My Life* shows, but I had to release my pain somehow. Joseph did it, so what says me, little Nicola. He intentionally placed his royal cup into the sack of his little brother Benjamin and accused his brothers of being unappreciative of his generosity. He accused them of stealing his cup, which he intentionally put into their sacks. He brought them back to his palace and just played mind games on them to release the pain and emotion bottled inside all these years. I had to do something.

After I did that, I calmed down and started to pray for forgiveness. I believe forgiveness, like grieving, is a process. I needed a power higher than me to help put the past behind me. I knew that until I forgave, those men still controlled my life remotely. There was no need to allow them to victimize me way after the fact. People like that are like snakes. A snake carries poison that does not kill it—it's fine with it on the inside of its body. By instinct, it releases the venom into an innocent victim and continues with its life like nothing ever happened. To me, continuing to carry the pain of something done to you is like holding the poison of a snake that moved on with its life and is hunting its next victim.

And this is how I received my spiritual healing. I cried out to God in the name of Jesus Christ, and He heard me. True, there is balm in Gilead, and HIS name is Jesus. He is the best healing anointing that I know. Psalm 34:18 says, "The Lord is near to the brokenhearted and saves the crushed in spirit." He promises to make beauty out of ashes and does just that.

Pain created a void inside of me that was filled with bitterness and hatred, and I needed to empty myself of those negative feelings and fill my heart with not just something better but somebody greater, and that person is Jesus. So today, I can genuinely say many are the afflictions of a righteous person, but the Lord delivers him out of them all.

What my enemies intended for evil was turned around for my good. I don't mind declaring it, but nothing can separate me from the love of Christ. Neither death nor life, neither angels nor demons, neither our fears for today nor our worries about tomorrow—not even the powers of hell can separate us from God's love. No power in the sky above or in the earth below. Indeed, nothing in all creation will ever be able to separate us from the love of God that is revealed in Christ Jesus our Lord.

ABOUT THE AUTHOR

Nicola C. Darlington is an emergent healing and deliverance pastor whose ministry is undergirded by a versatile intercessory lifestyle. She brings fresh revelatory teachings from the Hebraic Perspective, which challenges the mundane interpretation of the word of God. Pastor Nicola is one of the pastors of Jesus Nation World, headquartered in McDonough, Georgia. Additionally, she owns Darling Periods, which distributes non-toxic revolutionary sanitary products.

Her greatest satisfaction and the true testament to her ministry is the commitment she has to her family.

www.pastornicola.com

CHAPTER 3

Coming from a Place of Love

by Caroline Barrow

They say a woman's intuition is powerful and always on point—that incredible force you get when you can immediately sense something, whether good, bad, or indifferent. You know what works for you, you get that feeling in your core, or you are overcome with immense joy. Either way, you just know. Having lived on Mother Earth for over half a century, you are given many opportunities to experience that determined power. It is said that when you are shown something about someone, believe it the first time. If you choose not to accept it the first time, then proceed with caution. Most times, if you choose not to believe it and it happens again and again, it is more of a hobby rather than just a coincidence. Thankfully, it doesn't change who you are within.

As children, our parents will always tell us to be careful and vigilant of our surroundings. Not everyone you meet should be trusted immediately; get to know a person first. Keep your ears open and your eyes peeled. God gave us two ears so that we listen more than speak. Out there is not the safest place sometimes. Out there, meaning the real world. Your home is your sanctuary. Your home should be peaceful, happy, and a place you want to run back to.

My early days at home were in London, where I was born, lived, was educated, and started my career up until my mid-thirties. So, I have spent more than half of my life in the UK. But, also, during my early years, I spent quite a few of them living in Guyana, South America, where my parents were born. Our roots and foundation were formed in Guyana.

Guyana was a British colony before the country became independent on 26 May 1966. It meant all of the British ways were adopted initially during the era when I was born. The school system was the same; the teaching, training, examinations, and school gradings were all the same. This meant a great deal as I started my early years in education in Guyana and transitioned back to the UK at the beginning of secondary school. Although Guyana is in South America, it is part of the Caribbean Community (Caricom) and the West Indies. Known as a land of six races: Chinese, East Indians, Whites, African, Portuguese and Amerindian, it is bursting with culture, eco-tourism, and a flavorful array of foods.

The early years were some of my best years living all under the same roof with my parents and siblings in our beautiful modern home surrounded by lush gardens, trees bearing organic fruit, and large windows giving all the natural light you could handle. We lived a life of the haves versus the have-nots. The street is named after our family. Our housekeepers spent many years with our family, one notably until she retired, our beloved Ms. Carmen, head housekeeper in charge of our parents' belongings and the kitchen. Sister Barry, always a joy to talk to with her amazing stories, was in charge of assisting wherever she could, including washing the rice before it was cooked. Then there was Esther, who took care of us children, our rooms, clothes, hair, and the overall cleanliness of the house.

My parents were/are devoted Christians, which meant structure and routine, as in many Caribbean homes. Christian Brethren Church on the Public Road, East Bank Demerara, was our church back in those days. Every Sunday, without fail, that was where you would find our family. My dad sometimes preached when he wasn't traveling and, without a doubt, Sunday school every Sunday for the kids. Sundays also meant family dinner at the table, with the table being set by the kids and food laid out on the table like it was Thanksgiving or Christmas. No one was allowed to touch the food until my dad sat down at the head of the table and said grace, then it was OK to eat.

Our driver was present every day except Sundays when my dad would drive us around. The driver took the children to and from school and to all extracurricular activities like ballet, piano lessons, and violin. Our gardener kept the yard beautiful, and the trees bore fruit. He would pick the organic mangoes, carambola, guavas, and cashews off the tree and have them washed and ready for the family every day. Our security guard started work at sundown every night, usually around 9:00 p.m., and his sole job was to stay awake all night, keeping our house and grounds safe.

We also had a family farm in Timehri, Guyana, complete with a farmhouse spread over a few acres. We had chickens and fresh eggs, a vegetable garden full of limes, pineapples, and bora (greens) and sold turkeys in December, close to Christmas. Phew, those were the good old days, as they say.

By the very early 1980s, our family moved back to England, except for my dad, who stayed behind to run the family insurance business. At the time, Guyana's economy was in a tailspin pulling many of its citizens' living standards down with it. The government had banned certain preserved foods from being imported into the country, and other staples like wheat used for flour were scarce as the government could not afford the foreign exchange to buy them. Shortages of essential items like rice, peas, basic living regiments, and the way of life as we knew it was being compromised. My family decided to continue our lives and education in the land of our birth, England. My dad traveled to England every other month to be with the family. But, of course, he always traveled for work anyway, so this was something he was used to.

Moving back to the UK meant starting over as we did not own a home or a car, nor were we registered for school, and my mother did not have a job. Pretty much the opposite of being in Guyana as we went from being the haves to the have-nots within twenty-four hours. Yes, that is how life can change for you in an instant. What we did have was money saved and a lucrative business in Guyana. Moving from a five-bedroom, four-bathroom detached house with a driveway, garage, and landscaped yard, to a one-bedroom rental apartment was quite a change. My brother slept on two armchairs put together, my sister and I shared a double bed, my mom slept in a chair, and my other two sisters slept at the home of other family members. We did not have a driver or housekeepers. We cleaned our own surroundings and helped whenever we could.

The new school year was upon us starting that September. It was time to buckle up and get registered for our new school. But wait, no driver waited outside to take us to school; nope, we bought bus passes and rode the double-decker red bus to school in the chilly weather. We worked hard in class to keep our grades up as education, regardless of where we were, was always the number one priority in our household.

The holidays came around fast. Somehow, living at that slower pace in the sunshine in South America seems to give you more time during the day. It was the opposite in the UK; the days went much faster and seemed shorter. Outdoor activity was limited as the weather was much colder, the sunset was earlier and watching the many shows on TV was a family activity and something we did to pass the time. Clocks were set back by an hour in the fall, which seemed odd as I'd never experienced that in the Caribbean. I remember our first Christmas in England; my dad insisted that we have a traditional Christmas, which was always a big deal in our home. So, instead of spending the holidays in a one-bedroom apartment, my dad rented a three-bedroom house for us in time for our first Christmas. That was extremely special as it meant everyone being under the same roof for Christmas. My birthday is 31 December, so in my early years, I always got to celebrate my birthday with my family, which made it extra special. We started off New Year's Eve at church and would always ring in the new year at church. We found a Baptist church close to the new property in Sudbury, Middlesex, England, which became our church home.

Humble beginnings when I think back to the time of my early childhood. It all helped to shape and mold me into who I am today and how I conduct myself. As a teenager navigating London and making new friends, I seldom followed the crowd unless it was a festival or a parade.

I started my first job as a cashier at Safeway, a supermarket in Ealing Broadway, working each Saturday and earning GBP 10.00. I remember saving my wages for up to ten weeks to purchase a GBP 100.00 leather jacket from Portobello Market in London.

My friends at the time were more focused on leaving school because, at age sixteen, in the UK, you can fully emancipate yourself, leave school and home, and live independently if you can afford to. Many people from my high school did that without finishing school or graduating. Coming from a Caribbean household, that was unheard of. Education was one of the most important things my parents taught my siblings and me. I instill that same importance in my children today, and so far, it's working. In other words, you can do all things through Christ and education.

Although I had no choice but to finish school, I also went on to higher education, completing one year of A (Advanced) levels in Mathematics & Statistics and Economics. I took a year off to work and earn some money after my higher education and enrolled in university straight after to complete my four-year Bachelor of Arts with honors in Business/Leisure

Management (Major). I was the first of my siblings to graduate from university, a very proud moment for my family and me. It wasn't easy to focus with so many distractions, but I was (and still am) a very hard worker. Whatever I put my mind to, I like to complete to the best of my ability. Unfortunately, I am sometimes too much of a perfectionist. I remember losing a couple of friends along the way because I remained focused on my education and landed a job in the aviation industry before I finished college.

During my twenties, I experienced some of the most significant events that changed my life and shaped my life today. I started my career in aviation as I have a deep love for travel and all things tourism, cultures and traveling the world, meeting and talking to interesting people. While living in London, the gateway to Europe, you get a taste of many cultures and meet people from all over the world. I was once a tour guide in London while I was a student, which helped develop my love for the travel and tourism industry. My job afforded me many firsts, including traveling all over the world, sometimes in first class on long-haul flights to Ethiopia, Los Angeles, New York, Singapore, Thailand and almost every country in Europe. I also toured all over England, Scotland, Wales, and Northern Ireland.

In my mid-twenties, I was encouraged to enter a beauty pageant and won the title of Ms. Guyana UK. This meant a year in the entertainment industry, fulfilling my duties as the reigning beauty queen. I was featured in magazines in the UK, made appearances at many events and travelled to Guyana for TV appearances, philanthropy work, and giving back to the community and country of my roots. It was significant to compete in a pageant and win it at twenty-six, next to some eighteen and nineteen-year-olds. I

thought to myself, *if I don't do something like this now, I won't ever*, so I took that leap of fate, and it paid off.

As reigning queen for a year, I was invited to and attended many exquisite events, some with His Excellency, the High Commissioner in the UK for Guyana, spending time amongst diplomats and local celebrities.

That same year, 1997, when I won the pageant, was also the year Princess Diana died in a car accident in Paris. I remember coming home from an event and hearing it on the news in the early hours of the morning. Not many people were awake at the time, so I quietly made my way to a store, bought some flowers, and placed them at the gates of Buckingham Palace. It was surreal to sob for someone I only knew through the media. As the People's Princess and a beautiful soul, I admired Diana greatly for her love of life, love for her family, in particular her kids, and how she conducted herself in the public eye: fierce and poised with class and dignity. At the time of her death, I lived in Kensington W14, about fifteen minutes from Kensington Palace, which was her home while she was in London. I also laid flowers there and was one of many to line the streets in London as she made her final journey through the city.

In the last year of my twenties, I was pregnant with my first child, my daughter. My partner at the time asked me to move in as we were expecting a child together. We were not married and, in fact, had decided to go our separate ways just before I found out I was pregnant. So, there I was, pregnant in an already broken situationship. How would I tell my Christian parents that my life was about to change forever? Living with my partner made the news easier to disclose to my parents, so I agreed to move in and rent my place to tenants. Needless to say, this entire situationship did not work out, and we separated before my daughter was born. Then, on 30 December, after a shopping trip with one of my friends, my waters broke. Was it stress, was it anxiety, was it tension? I am not sure, but God knew best as the best place for me was the hospital under the care of the nurses.

I spent the night at the hospital and, the following day, was hooked up to the monitors to keep an eye on the baby. I remember seeing the monitors go blank a few times and the nurses telling me my daughter was in distress. It was all surreal as it was my thirtieth birthday, and I was about to undergo surgery for an emergency c-section. The nurses said my daughter would like to wish me a "Happy Birthday," so as I signed off on the paperwork and forms, I was being wheeled into the theater for my operation.

I began my thirties as a new mommy with a premature baby born six weeks early. My days at the beginning of 2000 were spent in a neonatal unit. Finally, two weeks in, the doctor gave me the all-clear so my daughter could go home. Thankful and grateful, I packed my stuff and left the hospital. I returned to the house, and with no help or care, the best place for us was with my family.

Having a newborn and a preemie meant being up almost twenty-four hours. The extra care, medicine, routine, schedule, and taking care of yourself were paramount. With the help of my family, I was able to do just that.

New single mom—new praying single mom—I was worried and excited at the same time. I thank God for the village I had to help raise my daughter, my supportive family and friends, my work life, and my career at the same company I started straight out of college.

The rest of my thirties held some of the best days of my life and some of the worst to date. My daughter and I travelled to many places, including Orlando, New York, Paris, Barcelona, Portugal, Washington, D.C., and Miami, on vacation and visiting family overseas. She had a passport at six months old, definitely a "travel baby."

I met my ex-husband in my mid-twenties on one of my trips to Washington, D.C. and didn't know that the guy my cousin introduced me to would eventually become my husband. He lived in Washington and traveled to London one day out of the blue to see me about two years after my daughter was born. Immediately there was a connection, and as the saying goes, the rest is history.

I spent half of my thirties in London, in a long-distance relationship and often travelled between London and Washington. After we decided to get married, I had the long road of applying for a fiancée visa and travelled to the US when it was approved. Emigrating to a new country and city was scary yet exciting as I welcomed my new life in the USA. I spent the rest of my thirties living in Washington, D.C.

I became pregnant with my son, who was also born in December; funny enough, he, too, was a couple of weeks early. He should have been born on 31 December, then we would all share the same birthday. My son brought an element of peace to the household, a joy to us all, including his big sister, who loved spending time with the new baby. Working full time (as breadwinner) and raising my two young kids, the strain and stress of everyday life in a new country with no support and family had its challenges. Although my marriage did not work due to irreconcilable differences, it turned out to be my best mistake. Some of my most poignant memories of being in D.C. involved spending time in court, going through a divorce and doing what was best for my children and me. If "*I didn't know my own strength*" was a person, it was me at that time.

Imagine being new to a country, a city, with no family and two young children, and left on my own, with an ex-husband who tried everything he could, along with his own village, to make me feel uncomfortable. But God...let me tell you about the God I serve; He is such a forgiving God.

The night before our wedding, something came over me, and I had second thoughts about the marriage. That intuition I talked about earlier in this chapter is what I felt in my core. But, as the wedding was overseas and so many of our family and friends had traveled to be with us, I could not let anyone down, so I took the hit and let myself down and went ahead with it. God is so forgiving; He gave me my wonderful healthy baby boy, then revealed that this marriage was not for me, and it was time to leave. God is always on time, believe me.

They say life begins at forty, and I am living proof that it does. My job was going well, and things had settled in Washington, but the life I wanted for my children was not the same as living in a two-bedroom apartment on 14th Street with no outside space for about $2000 in rent, another $1600 for daycare, and a high cost of living. It was draining both financially and emotionally. My cousin lived in Atlanta and encouraged me to look into Atlanta homes, schools, and the cost of living and compare the two cities. It was a no-brainer. We decided that moving the family to Atlanta would be best, which meant getting approval from the D.C. courts and transferring from my job. Thankfully my job was flexible enough for me to work remotely in Atlanta. So, at the end of 2012, we moved to Atlanta, Georgia.

Being a single parent (by choice) has its pros and cons. Some people become single parents by default or by a situation. In my case, it was both, so I had to make it work and went into straight survivorship mode. I knew I had the strength to pull it off but trust me, there were many, many days and many, many moments when I felt that I couldn't do it anymore. It was so hard trying to juggle a successful career in Account Management with two young children and a new home in a new city. There were new ways of doing things, navigating the policies of the land, meeting new friends, and trusting babysitters, as I didn't have any family or a "village" to babysit.

Living in the south has its perks. The weather is sunny most of the year, and I love how close Georgia is to Florida, so if I need more sun in the winter, I can head over to the Sunshine State in just a few hours. Not long after moving to Atlanta, I bought our first home. The house was built from the ground up. I chose my lot and watched it being built, a beautiful spacious home which reminded me of my home back in Guyana during those early years. My kids made friends in the neighborhood, their schools were close by, and we formed a special bond and friendship with local parents. We were receiving blessing after blessing.

I joined many groups and formed a sisterhood with a few American "divas," some of my "girls" here in the ATL. We spent many Thanksgivings and Christmases with them, birthdays, and outings with or without partners. We periodically get together and are connected within a text group. We still plan trips today and, in fact, just returned from a weekend in the Blue Ridge Mountains catching up with each other. Life seems to go so fast these days, so giving people flowers when they can smell them is very important.

I was also pleased to know that Atlanta had a sizeable Caribbean community and a carnival, a chance to enjoy my culture. I remember the first year I moved to Atlanta, there was one big carnival in downtown Atlanta. I took the kids to the parade, and we loved seeing the culture, the carnival bands, eating the cuisine, seeing the flags of the Caribbean nations, and getting into the festival village and rejoicing with the crowd.

The following year, there were only two bands, and we couldn't figure out what was happening after such a massive explosion of culture the previous year. Only the festival village was in full effect. We left, very disappointed, as we were looking forward to a large parade, food, and bands like we had experienced the year prior.

Steelpan, Calypso, and Soca music are some of my favorite genres of music which I love to hear at Caribbean parades and events. Music generally makes me happy and takes me to my own world. I used to deejay at some of our house parties in my late teens and early twenties. Constantly buying new music on vinyl and later on compact discs when they were around. Nowadays, I have various playlists and listen to my favorite genres on the go via my phone, tablet and in the car.

With the rise and rise of social media and a growing social "friend" list and groups, I was able to find a lot of the Caribbean culture in Atlanta and some events and lounges around town. I joined many Facebook groups and connected with people of similar cultures from our Caribbean nations, including Guyana. It was a great feeling to connect with people who love the culture.

Playing mas (short for masquerade) is a happy, joyous experience where participants dress in costumes, masks, feathers, lots of feathers and other disguises and dance on the streets throughout a parade route. The first time I played mas as an adult was in Atlanta, in the DeKalb Carnival for a band called Madd Colors Carnival Band. That was amazing. The colors of my costume, the feathers and all the joy I got from playing mas were fantastic. So great that the next opportunity to play mas, I did it again and again. In addition to the parade, Atlanta carnival season also comes with many events and parties, a.k.a. "fetes." So, it was no surprise that my friends and I labelled the week-long celebrations as #teamnosleep after being out late at most events and getting up early the next day to participate in breakfast parties, day parties, evening events and the carnival itself. J'ouvert, also part of the festival, meaning "break day," signifies the start of carnival and celebrates emancipation from slavery. For J'ouvert, our bodies are covered in colored paints or mud, sometimes pitch oil, and like the carnival, you dance in the streets and rejoice as an expression of liberation and freedom.

The last year of my forties was the year of the pandemic, which brought the world to a standstill. I was one of the millions affected head-on in many ways. I was working in the aviation industry, which basically was forced to shut down at the beginning of the pandemic. The pandemic led to several events and outings being cancelled, and everyone was advised to stay home. So, from being an all-around busybody with numerous projects, I found myself at home with no job and my e-commerce business not doing very well. I also worked with my fifth-grader, homeschooling, in the last few weeks of elementary school.

Just as school ended and the summer break began, I received the most devasting news ever that my dad's health was starting to deteriorate. My parents were home in Guyana. I remember the words from my mother like it was yesterday, frantically asking us, the siblings, to stand by via our group chat as she updated us with news concerning his health, the doctor by his bedside and everyone I know praying. Ironically, just a few days after video-calling my mom and seeing my dad, I quietly cried all by myself as he looked frail. I did fear for the worst then, not knowing that three days later, the worst thing that could ever happen to our family occurred, and we lost the king of our castle, the head of our family; my beloved dad was gone.

I am still thankful to this day that I was fortunate to have seen him in February 2020 when I visited our home, his beloved home in Guyana, with my son. I saw his smile, held his hand, and his warm embrace, and those precious memories will live on in my heart forever. Yet, it still feels surreal knowing he is not here on Earth with us. He was a significant loss to the world and Guyana, the country he loved. I know at some stage, as we, the children, get older, it means our elders and parents get older, still. Yes, it is inevitable, but you are never prepared when the worst happens. It does not get any easier as you get older. Losing a parent is devasting beyond words, but my comfort is that my dad was a devoted Christian. He always used to say that he knew where he was going, Heaven, so that gave him the peace he needed on Earth.

I spent the downtime in 2020 studying for my real estate license. Education has always been important to me, so getting the chance to study and become knowledgeable in a different field was rewarding. I've always had a deep interest in properties and property management. I bought my first property straight out of college after starting my first job in my mid-twenties. Since then, I've bought and sold properties in the UK and the US for years, so getting licensed just made sense.

People say you only live once, but if you do it right, once is enough. I am still a work in progress. Happiness starts within, love starts within, and the willingness to get up and make a difference every day is on you. Nowadays, I live my life on purpose with integrity and class. I am so happy to know that I am accountable only to myself and God, professionally and personally. I have had people come into my life who are supposed to be there and are still, and I've had people who were only supposed to be there for a season or reason. When that season is over, there is no reason for them to continue to be there, perhaps from a distance but not up close and personal.

For the ones still in my life, thank you for the "I love yous," the flowers, the laughter, the joy, the stories, the vibe, and the beautiful memories we're making together. The ones who are no longer there, thank you for the lessons, the mistakes, the regrets, the dishonesty, you helped me to know what I don't need in my future so that the remainder of my time here can be peaceful with positive energy around me.

As a female December Capricorn, and yes, it makes a difference, we are naturally charitable and willing to go beyond whatever is being asked of us to help. I will always show empathy for others and literally put myself in their shoes to understand their need or ask. I have helped and supported many to date, mentored young girls, and have generously given emotionally and financially without asking or expecting anything in return. I've noticed that when I'm in need of the same, not many are there to support or help in the same way. I must show up for myself now. My goal is to live my life purposefully and unapologetically for me and mine.

Somethings I learned when I turned fifty:

- You just can't make real friends with fake people. If they are not genuine and coming from a place of love, I'm not interested in friendship, relationship, situationship or entanglement. I don't care how often they apologize and say I love you; I value you. If it's not for me, I don't want it.
- You have to sit back and observe people, things and situations. Not everything needs a reaction from you. Be patient; they will reveal themselves eventually.
- You must trust your intuition. If something doesn't feel right about somebody or a situation, don't waste your time trying to deny it. Your intuition is powerful and most often spot on!! That force is coming directly from the universe.

- The older you get, the less you feel the need to be included, understood or accepted. So, maintain patience as God works quietly for you and will guide you to be better.

The glory of God has been present throughout my life and has guided my decisions. Therefore, I place high regard on standards and maintain certain boundaries, as protecting my peace of mind is essential. I can't wait to see what's in store for me this next decade. So far, it has begun with nothing but love, happiness, and positivity.

ABOUT THE AUTHOR

Ms. Caroline Barrow is a British native of Guyanese descent residing in Atlanta, GA. She is a dedicated professional with extensive experience in Account Management, Marketing, Travel, Human Resources and Compliance. Caroline has worked for many international companies in the aviation, media and travel industries and is a host and executive consultant at Caribbean Life TV & Radio, a worldwide online network based in Atlanta. Throughout her career, she has received numerous rewards and recognitions for her work, dedication, passion, and drive.

She graduated with honors from the University of West London with a Bachelor of Arts degree in Leisure Management. She is a licensed Realtor ® with Century 21 in the State of Georgia and a member of the Cobb Association of Realtors ®, the Georgia Realtors ® Association and the National Association of Realtors ®. She has traveled the world with many more countries still to explore.

Caroline was crowned Ms. Guyana UK in 1997 and has since represented her heritage and love for Guyana on numerous occasions. She loves all things Caribbean, including food, culture, weather, music, and entertainment.

https://www.instagram.com/sweetcarolinebee/
https://www.facebook.com/cazzybeebee
https://www.tiktok.com/@cazzybee

CHAPTER 4

Rejection from Within

by CasSandra D. Belton

Early Childhood Education

Statistics say, "On average, the earliest memories that people can recall point back to when they were just two-and-a-half years old."[1] I don't recall back to age two, but I do remember starting the first grade in Apalachicola, Florida while living with my maternal grandmother at the age of five. My first-grade teacher was Mrs. Inez Baker. After completing the first grade, I moved back to Maryland with my parents and attended Randolph Village Elementary School on Central Avenue. I remember walking down the hill from my house to the bus stop with my neighbors

---

[1] https://www.sciencedaily.com, Jun 14, 2021

and catching the bus. There are a few other things that I remember. The school was across the street from a drive-in theater, and I was in the Scuba Diving Reading Club, where I received numerous certificates. One particular day, a helicopter landed on the field while the children were in the parking lot. Captain 20, from a local TV station, came to visit our school. Why? Now, that, I don't remember. But I remember that all the school children were excited to go home and tell their families.

Between a Rock and a Hard Place

The children at school were different from the children who lived on my street. The ones who lived on my street were like family, and we often visited each other's homes. Not only did we walk to the bus stop together, but we also played in each other's yard, and when it came to real backyard fun, my family was the only house in the neighborhood with an above-ground swimming pool. I guess this was an added benefit of a two-parent household. My dad, Edwin, was a foreman with Burton and Robinson Construction Company, and my mother, Odella, was a beautician at Etna's Beauty Salon.

One day, my dad arrived home from work and backed up his company construction truck into our front yard. He and one of his coworkers pushed a large boulder off the truck. He later cleaned it with acid and told us not to touch it, or it would burn a hole in our hands. True or not, I believed him.

On another day, while playing with my oldest brother in the front yard, I called him my stepbrother. I may not have known what it meant, but I remember a classmate introducing me to her stepbrother before boarding my school bus one day. My mother heard me from inside the house and called me in. Well, that one word caused me to get the worst discipline I had ever received. Why me? What did I do? Could we have just talked about it? I guess not. That type of discipline would have never happened at Grandma E's house. I could hardly wait until it was time to visit her again.

Family Vacation

We never went on a real family vacation, so every time we went to Grandma E's house in Florida, I considered that to be our family vacation. It was like going to the country because I didn't have to wear shoes, do any chores, do any homework, or worry about what time it was. I was there to have fun and visit Grandma E. I loved when she would call me into her room to thread the sewing needles. I thought that was odd. Grandma E didn't have running hot water, so we took turns heating water on the stove and pouring it into the tub to take a bath. I thought that was strange, also. She had a fig tree and a Japanese plum tree in the backyard. You haven't had a real fig until you have pulled one off of a tree. Pecan trees were up and down the alleys, Mr. Bryant had a pear tree on the side of his house, and we could always go to Mrs. Baker's house to buy some scuppernongs. We could leave the house and play all day as long as we were home in time for dinner when the Catholic School bell rang at 6:00 p.m. We were often seen running down the street just to land on Grandma E's porch as the bell hit that last strike. After spending a week with Grandma E, we loaded up the car. While sitting in the back seat, Grandma E asked what I wanted for the trip home. That was a rhetorical question because she knew I wanted her oatmeal raisin cookies. She had my tin can ready. There were layers of cookies wrapped in wax paper. To this day, my favorite cookie is oatmeal raisin, although it's not Grandma E's cookies. With my tin can in hand, Grandma E and Geronimo were standing on the front porch, and all of a sudden, Geronimo started jumping and yelling, "I don't want to go back! I don't want to go back." Grandma E responded, "Leave him here!" Did my parents even discuss this? My mother agreed, and that was the end of it. We started our road trip back home with Grandma E and Geronimo waving goodbye from the front porch. What would it feel like once we got home and Geronimo wasn't there? I guess the only difference would be that he wouldn't get to hear all of the arguing and fighting that went on behind closed doors.

Arguing and Fighting

Adults always say what goes on in the house stays in the house; unfortunately, their fights often went outside, and our neighbors were very aware of them. With the Hilliard family living next door and their three children being our closest friends, they knew. The Johnston family lived directly across the street from our house, and they knew. Their daughter was our babysitter. Although their son lived in his parent's basement, he didn't know much. The one who sat in the window rocking back and forth, known to us as the Grandmother, was a sweet little old lady who witnessed a lot. On one occasion, Daddy was really fed up with Odella's arguing. He could barely get in the house from work, and an argument would start. On this particular day, he obtained the jack from the car. Although I didn't see him hit her with it, I remember her having a gash on her head. I was so scared because she had to go to the hospital.

Our other friends, Deborah, Joyce, and Chucky, were down the street from the Johnstons. We always played cricket in their backyard, so they knew about the problems in my household. At the bottom of the hill was the Smith family, who had only one child named Ricky. They may not have known a lot, but they also knew there were problems.

While attending Randolph Village Elementary School in the fifth grade, Odella decided to make her move and get out of the relationship. As a habit, we always came out of school and caught the school bus. But this day, Odella was outside and picked us up in the bus loading zone. Needless to say, we didn't go home. Instead, we went to a new place to call home. We left the house with the swimming pool in the backyard and the big rock in the front yard and were transported to an apartment building. This would become our new normal: a two-bedroom apartment in Washington, D.C. Unfortunately, we didn't get the opportunity to say goodbye to our long-time friends. Who knows what lies ahead in this new neighborhood.

The Dog's Owner

On the first day of moving into the neighborhood, we were told to go outside and play. In this neighborhood, where would we play? The front of the building was dirt and the street, and the back was an alley. With less traffic in the alley, that's where we played. Up and down, and at the end of the alley.

I saw honeysuckers in a yard hanging on the right. So, loving things sweet, I decided to get honeysuckers from the tree but didn't notice that a dog came with this property. I didn't see it, but it saw me. And you guessed it. The dog bit me on the inside of my right thigh. After making it back home, I was transported to the hospital and obtained the first of many rabie shots. It would be one shot in the navel every morning for fourteen days.

When we arrived back home, my mother called the police. I got to ride in the back seat of the police car down the alley so I could show him where it happened. The question was whether or not the dog was up to date on his rabie shots. According to the police, the dog's owner disowned even having a dog, so my mother assumed the dog was not properly vaccinated. That was terrible news for me. I had always heard that these shots were very painful. And upon receiving each shot, I cried every single visit. But one thing is for sure, I remembered my last visit.

I was taken there by my dad. And on this visit, I did not cry. Because I didn't shed tears on my last visit, they gave me a handful of lollipops. Was it because I didn't cry, or was it because it was my last visit? One thing that made me happy was that my daddy took me to that last appointment.

Now it was time to go to my new school. Davis Elementary, here I come. It would be the second school I attended, and I was still in the fifth grade. Different neighborhood, different school, but the same father.

Dropped off at Grandma E's

Now that my father, Edwin, knew where we lived, he tried to visit us often. But, we were instructed not to open the door; he would knock and eventually kick on the apartment door. So, Odella moved us once again. But this time, she took us to Grandma E's house—all the way to Florida.

With Geronimo and my cousin, Jeanna, already living there, Grandma E had a house full of grandchildren. I was happy just being there. I was still in the fifth grade and enrolled in Chapman Elementary School, my third school for my fifth-grade year. It wasn't a problem because there was no fighting, screaming or hollering at Grandma E's house. Odella then returned to Washington, D.C. I made a lot of new friends while attending school in Florida and was involved in a lot of extracurricular activities. I participated in Spelling Bees, was in gymnastics, and even learned how to crochet in my art classes. Crocheting is something that I still do. Those two years went by quickly, but Odella returned, and it was time to return to the city.

Moving Back to the City

After finally completing Fifth Grade, Sixth Grade and half of Seventh Grade in Florida, Odella finally returned to Grandma E's house to pick me up along with my two younger brothers. I will always cherish those fond memories. Finally, after two years, we went back to D.C., but not with Geronimo.

Once we arrived in D.C., the new apartment was approximately two miles south of our other apartment. Once again, I was in a different school district. Where would I go for Middle School? Just follow the crowd.

The students led us to Kelly Miller Jr. High School, referred to as "The University." I was placed in the homeroom of Mrs. James. I loved everything about my teacher, especially because she accepted me as her own. I eventually started calling her "Ma" for the next two and a half years until I graduated from the ninth grade. I did this so much that other classmates thought she was my biological mother. If I could find her today, I would be so elated. I pray that it's not too late. She provided encouragement away from home.

At home, I was degraded. I would hear words like, "God doesn't like ugly, and He ain't too crazy about pretty." I was very familiar with the first part of this statement; however, the second half was my mom's added touch. Being fair-skinned, I was also called "high yella." I never heard any of this language while attending Kelly Miller Jr. H.S.

My Classmate's Mother

At Kelly Miller Jr. H.S., also known to all the students as "The University," another student named Deb recognized my last name. One day she felt the need to tell her mom about the new student in her class. Her mom was dating a gentleman with my last name. Yes, it was my dad. How ironic. My brothers and I had been gone for approximately two years, and Edwin was about to reunite with his children. And that he did, but secretly.

One day he drove to the school, sat outside, and watched me walk home. There was no disturbance at all. But, by doing this, he would find out where the new apartment was. How many days did he follow me? I don't know. But one day, he finally spoke to me. I was thrilled, and so was he. I couldn't go home and tell Odella. It wasn't immediate, but I told her I saw Daddy. I don't remember her response or reaction. But eventually, he started picking us up over the weekends. Going to his apartment in Maryland was fun. We often went to the go-kart tracks and to see the roller derby games with Sonja Sims and Little Richard, who were roller derby all-stars. On many occasions, dinner would be from McDonald's, and we were okay with that. He occasionally allowed us to walk to McDonald's on George Palmer Highway with instructions to come right back. He trusted me, even when Odella didn't. His apartment was nice, quiet and peaceful. Therefore, I had peace when visiting him and peace at school.

Living in the Projects

Being settled in school was good, and being an active member of the church down the street was great. Having friends in my neighborhood was fantastic. But for some strange reason, we were about to move again. Who moves to the projects while in high school? I thought people grew up in the projects and then moved out. Kenilworth, here we come.

We went from a house with a swimming pool, to an apartment, to another apartment, then into the projects. That seemed backwards, not to mention we lived on the third floor. In our new apartment, things didn't change much.

Coming home from school one day, I walked up to the third floor, opened the door with my key, and as soon as I stepped foot into the apartment, Odella started beating me with a broom. What adult hides behind the door in their own residence? What was this for? Wait! What have I done now? This was crazy. I couldn't wait to leave.

Being in the eleventh grade and living there, I started thinking about going to college just to get out of the house. But I had never thought about going to college before. So, I asked Odella about college money, and her exact words were:

"I ain't got no college money for you!

You betta get a government job with some benefits."

That stuck! Considering I was a grade ahead of myself, I went to school to inquire about my credits and where I stood for graduation. I was on track to have more than enough credits, allowing me to work part-time after becoming a senior. So, during my Senior year, I started working after school on October 4, 1976, until I graduated on June 6, 1977.

Of all the places in the world to work, I started at the Internal Revenue Service (IRS) at 10th and Pennsylvania Avenue. This was, and still is, a powerful intersection. On one side of the street was the Department of Justice (DOJ), and on the other was the Federal Bureau of Investigation (FBI). I worked part-time at the IRS until I presented my high school diploma after graduation. Afterwards, I immediately became a full-time employee. I am now employed with a government job, with benefits.

The '77 Thunderbird

It was 1976; I was sixteen years old and classified as a senior in high school. That alone was a milestone and extremely exciting. I did not attend a regular high school. Instead, I attended Chamberlain Vocational High School, where my main focus was secretarial skills. I was enrolled in a Clerk Typist homeroom, and Ms. Wylie was our shop teacher. After the first semester, I received A/B Honor Roll and was transferred to Mrs. Turner's homeroom, where my primary focus would be on Stenography. That career would earn me more than a clerk typist career.

Mrs. Turner became another one of my mother figures. To many, she was known to be mean to her students because we were on the outside, looking In. After being in her class for a while, I became very familiar with her and what she wanted for her students. She only wanted the best for everyone who was in her class. I may not have been the fastest using the stenography machine, but I think I did pretty darn good.

Attending Chamberlain and then learning how to drive was a privilege. Being taught driving lessons by my dad was even more exciting. He owned a green and white Thunderbird, and after getting my learner's permit, he let me practice every weekend. After obtaining my driver's license, I was even allowed to get the car on Fridays after he came home from work, and I kept it until Sunday evenings. He knew where I was going when I kept the T-bird—to church and back home. Driving to school during the week was not an option. I am very proud to say that my daddy taught me excellent driving skills. I say this every single week because he is no longer here to see how his teaching paid off (but he's not the only one who passed away). After almost forty years in the secretarial field, I am now a professional bus operator for American Disabilities Act passengers, and I owe it all to him. Thank you, Daddy!

Grandma E Passes Away

In the summer of 1980, the worst thing imaginable happened. Grandma E passed in August. After attending her funeral, there would be no more trips to Florida. No more going to the laundromat to carry the clothes, helping her hang them on the line, and propping them up. No more of her famous oatmeal raisin cookies. No more sleeping in on Saturdays. She did things before the crack of dawn. No more threading the sewing needle for her while she sat in the rocking chair, looking out the window, watching people pass by. No more heating water on the stove to pour in the tub, just to take a bath. That's what we had to do. On Saturday nights, the young people went to the Recreation Center, known as "The Rec." We went home after The Rec closed. Grandma E would have the room heated until we fell asleep.

Then the kerosene heaters would go out until she lit them first thing in the morning before we woke up. No more running behind the mosquito truck. No more scratching her scalp. No more shooting marbles. You don't play marbles; you shoot marbles. No more picking Japanese plums and figs in the backyard. No more selling pecans in a brown paper bag and waiting for the pecan man to come around to purchase them. No more going to the Snack Bar, where there were a lot of snacks, a pool table, and a dance floor in the back, in the dark. Without Grandma E, these things were but memories that would last forever. She never got to see many things, like being escorted down the aisle as the grandmother of the bride.

My Wedding Day

After Grandma E passed, I was proposed to and accepted. Although I was to be the bride, I had limited say regarding the festivities to follow the ceremony. The wedding reception was being funded by you know who. Odella! I would have had my reception at my church. However, she chose a separate location that would suit her and her guests' needs, including an open bar. That was not my choice, and neither was the menu. One thing I had control over was my cake. I had never seen a square wedding cake which was my cake of choice.

One thing that really disturbed me was that my father was not allowed to give me away. How could she have been controlling all those years? Geronimo was informed by Odella that his assignment was to walk me down the aisle and give me away. She even had verbiage for his response to the officiating preacher. "Who gives this bride away?" Geronimo was instructed to say, "Ms. Fryer and I." What the heck? If I had known in 1981, what I learned in October 2015, this would have never happened. My dad would have never been sitting in the audience as an invited guest. My brothers were in sky-blue suits with dark blue collars, and Edwin was in a brown suit sitting in the audience. Looking back, I can only imagine how heartbroken he felt. Arguing with Odella would have caused a scene, and he would have never done that to me. That would have been an unhealthy situation for him and for me.

Cancer Diagnosis

Edwin became ill and was later moved to California by his siblings. When someone dear to you passes, you will never forget where you were or your last conversation. We were still living in the projects on Kenilworth Avenue when the phone rang, and Odella yelled, "Get the phone!" My daddy was calling me from California. Although our conversation was brief, I remember it like it was yesterday. I told him that he sounded like himself. Out of all the things he went through, now I understand. For example, when you are in a marriage, be truthful from the very beginning. If not, there will be consequences that will cost you. Although he was looked upon as the untruthful partner, he was actually the truthful one.

After being diagnosed with cancer, Edwin died on January 2, 1991. His death occurred around some very popular dates in the family. My youngest brother's birthday is January 1st, my birthday is January 4th, and my daughter's birthday is January 11th. My church family collected an offering and presented it to me so I could attend my father's funeral, not alone, but with all three of my children. To this day, when I'm up late, in memory of my dad, I shut everything down at 12:17 a.m. in honor of his birthday, December 17, 1935. Being a single parent, this was one lemon that I had to turn into lemonade because life goes on after a loved one's death.

One Check Away

Being a single parent, years went by quickly, and difficult things, including losing my apartment, continued to happen. My income wasn't enough to pay for my children's Clinton Christian Academy tuition and my rent. I missed one child support check, and that did it. I was actually one check away from being homeless. Then, I received a call at work from my neighbor that my furniture was being put outside. I contacted my supervisor and my carpool mate and went home.

Odella and a couple of my friends were there. Someone had rented a U-Haul truck and put my belongings on it while Odella told people about my missing child support check. I was so embarrassed. After packing the truck, my carpool rider invited us to stay in her den. Odella's place was not an option.

We stayed with her for approximately three to four days until the closing of my new home. Being legally married but separated for many years, my house was in Odella's name to prevent my soon-to-be ex-husband from gaining anything in the divorce. The house was small, but it was mine. I was there for a few years before moving to California to be around my dad's side of the family. Although I located a renter, Odella was not happy; I was no longer under her control. I departed on October 27, 1994, at 6:00 a.m. I moved into my new apartment in San Leandro, CA, and my telephone number was 276-9410 (27th day @ 6:00 a.m. in the 94th year in the 10th month). This was my confirmation that this move was meant to be.

West Coast Bound

My church was so excited about my move to California that they held a Going Away Service in my honor. People from my past were in attendance, even my high school teacher, Mrs. Turner from Chamberlain Vocational High School. She spoke of things I'd done in her Stenography class, including the note that I wrote on the stenograph machine, "You hit on people like you are their mother. If you hit me, I'm going to knock you out the window, and you are going to fly like the 'Flying Nun!'" She knew the personalities of her students and knew it was from me. The entire church laughed so hard. Prior to her passing, I always visited her on my home visits.

Odella was the last speaker. She said, "Since her relief driver can't make it, I'm going to be her relief driver." What? I stood there in complete silence because I was in total disbelief and in complete shock. I'm moving to get away from you, and you're now telling all these people that you are going with me.

We arrived in San Leandro, CA, on October 30, 1994, and spent time with family at my aunt's apartment. I was so tired and went to bed early. I flew Odella back to D.C. the very next day. Later that day, I was asked by my aunt, "Why does your mom talk about you so bad?" My response was, "What? Really?" For her, it was all about a free trip to California. She received a free trip to California, knowing that she was going to eventually pay me back with the selling of my home, which was my investment property. It was still in her name because the divorce had not yet occurred.

She Sold My House

A couple of years later, while talking with my aunt, some information slipped out her mouth, "Your mom sold your house." I asked her over and over again until she repeated what I thought

I had heard. I had no clue. All because I was no longer under her control. Many months later, as if this wasn't enough, my aunt asked me to type a letter stating that she was removing a few of my cousins and me from the property in Panama City, FL. The property in Panama City was my inheritance from my dad's mother. I immediately responded, "Why would I do that?" Then, silence filled the room. Edwin always reminded me that I had property in Panama City. Eventually, our names were illegally removed from the property as heirs. Here I go again, losing another house because of my so-called family. Eventually, I had to let that go because my children were my main focus.

Morehouse College and Georgia State University

Odella knew what was happening in my children's lives, although she hadn't spoken to me in years. I was excited about my youngest son graduating from Morehouse College in 2009. I ordered everything from invitations to a large banner to hang across the front porch. I received word from my aunt, Edwin's baby sister, that Odella said she wasn't invited. The invitations had not arrived yet. When the invitations finally arrived, I put everything together and labeled the envelopes, and they were mailed one month before graduation. Yes, one was sent to Odella, but she was a no-show.

And then, in 2008, my one and only daughter attended Georgia State University and became very popular. In 2008, she crowned Ms. Black and Gold for the Alpha Fraternity. In 2010, she was voted Homecoming Queen. She went down in history as the last Homecoming Queen during basketball season and was crowned the first Homecoming Queen for their first football season. I created everything, including a banner for everyone to sign at her party. All invitations were labeled and mailed out one month before graduation. Odella was a no-show again! I would never treat her the way she treated me. My dad's side of the family still considered her as family when it came to funerals.

Panama City, FL

When Edwin's aunt, my great-aunt, passed away, my daughter and I drove four hours to attend the funeral. I was still trying to do the right thing, so I stopped by Odella's house just to say hello. I wouldn't dare go to her city and not visit her. I pulled up to her house but didn't see her car outside, so I called from my cell phone. Odella answered the phone and invited us in. My daughter and I exited the car, stepped inside, and my daughter was beginning to sit in the recliner when Odella came out of her bedroom and said, "I was just leaving." I looked at my daughter, and we walked out of the house and got back into the rental car. Odella came out, locked her door, got in a car parked in front of her door and pulled off. We sat there in disbelief. So, we went down the street to the beach and made the most of that hour.

When it was time to attend my great-aunt's funeral, we were all at the house, wearing white as instructed, but we hadn't heard from Odella. She had a seat in one of the family cars because they still considered her family. I was asked to call her. I did but got no answer. One of the other family members called and received no response. We finally loaded up in cars and headed to the funeral home.

Wouldn't you know it? Odella was standing at the door in black, passing out funeral programs. Walking in, two-by-two, Odella on my side, I asked her why she didn't come to the house because we were waiting for her. The stare into my eyes was there, but there was no response. She handed funeral programs to those in front of me and those behind me. She said not a word! My daughter was shocked. Rejected again. Did she not come to the house because I was attending the funeral? This was my great-aunt by blood. She was my dad's aunt. If Odella became ill, I would never treat her like she has treated me. I would lay everything aside and be there.

On the Way to the Hospital

Word reached me that Odella became ill, and since she didn't communicate with three of her children, I informed Geronimo that, according to her doctor, she was not supposed to be driving. It took him approximately one year to get her from Florida to Georgia, where he lives.

Late one evening, I received a call from Geronimo telling me he was following Odella in an ambulance. I inquired as to what had happened. He explained that while at work, he kept calling his house but didn't get an answer. When he got home, Odella was asleep in the chair. He fixed dinner and tried to wake her up but was unsuccessful. He called 911. They came and discovered that her blood sugar was low and she was slipping into a diabetic coma. I told him to call me once he heard something at the hospital and that I'd be headed that way first thing in the morning. I didn't receive a call, so I called him when I woke up. He said everything was fine, and they were releasing her from the hospital. I was going to make my way to the hospital, although I'm sure she would have said, "What are you doing here?" That statement would have crushed me, and I would have left the room and found somewhere to sit down and take it all in.

You Better Sit Down

In October 2015, we were about to have our first family reunion on Grandma E's side of the family. A Facebook page was created, and when the banner was uploaded, I noticed Grandma E and her two younger sisters did not have the same maiden name. So, I contacted my cousin Jeanna, who informed me that Grandma E had a different father. While still on the phone, I asked, "What else is there that I don't know?" And at that very moment, Jenna said, "So, I guess you don't know?" And I said, "Know what?" She said, "You better sit down."

Jeanna reminded me that my mom and dad used to fight a lot when we were growing up. Then she hit me with Odella's secret. Jenna recalled hearing my parents fighting during the night when we were supposed to be asleep at the house with the boulder in the front yard and the swimming pool in the backyard. She heard Edwin screaming, "I know that boy's not mine! I know he's not mine!" And there you have it! All these years after calling Geronimo my stepbrother in elementary school because I was introduced to my classmate's stepbrother, Odella assumed that I knew her life-long secret. I was only a child. I didn't even know what stepbrother meant.

Is it that Odella didn't like me because I reminded her of her guilt? The fact that she wasn't able to raise her first-born child, the child she had out of wedlock, the child that she told Edwin, was his, the child that she had in November 1958, before getting married on Valentine's Day in 1959.[2] Grandma E, Edwin and Odella all took her secret to their graves.

After learning of her secret, I did as Jeanna instructed and did not let Odella know that I knew her secret because I could cause her to become deathly ill or even have a heart attack. I definitely didn't want that to happen. So, Geronimo had no clue until I self-published my first book, *There's Purpose in My Pain,* in 2016.

Call to Action

Psalm 27:10 declares, "When my father and my mother forsake me, Then **the LORD will take care of me. (NASB) I** am a living witness that **F-A-M-I-L-Y** doesn't always mean **F**ather **A**nd **M**other; **I L**ove **Y**ou. I had to learn at an early age that a testimony doesn't come without a test, and victory doesn't come without trials and tribulation. But I never thought that it would come from my own family. In order to get the strength to go on, I had to trust God. I endured each test and trial to help you. Yes, you. This chapter was written with you in mind. Each step is just that, a step. It is designed to lead you in the right direction of trusting the one who knows your destiny. If I had not gone through the verbal and physical abuse I experienced in my childhood, I would have nothing to share with you. I am stronger because of it. It wasn't easy, but it was necessary. Why? So that I could encourage you today.

---

[2] www.ancestry.com

Whatever your life experiences have been, they were necessary for you to encourage the next person. I encourage you to hold on. God said in His Word that He would never leave you. It's time for you to move on, regardless of who hurt you; it's time for you to pick yourself up regardless of your past circumstances. It had to happen to get me to this point. You have been chosen to pass the torch of encouragement. God has you, just like He had me. I have the victory, and so do you!

ABOUT THE AUTHOR

CasSandra D. Belton became a multipreneur after working in the Federal Government and several law firms from Washington, D.C., to Silicon Valley, CA, for over thirty-seven years.

This dedicated single mother of three children started several businesses, including Ardnassac's Uneek Kreations, LLC, Uneek Shape, Primerica Financial Services, We Rock Black Socks, Organizing Made Easy 4 U, Step-by-Step Line Dancing Classes, and A Single Mom's W.O.W. ("Words of Wisdom"). Her goal is to develop Ardnassac's Uneek Kreations, LLC into a brand that will encompass the entire United States of America with her freestyle crocheting and her Ardnassas'c 365 Salve®, for which a Certificate from the U.S. Patent and Trademark Office for a Federal Registration was granted in September 2021.

With Ardnassac being CasSandra spelled backwards, this Salve helps remove scars from burns, cuts, eczema, and old and new surgical scars.

CasSandra's most impressive achievements thus far have been as the Announcement Secretary, for years, at her local church in Washington, D.C., working on voluminous U.S. patents for inventors all over the world while working in Silicon Valley, CA, and being ordained as the first female deacon at a large church in Jonesboro, GA.

One quirky fact about her is that she loves to go to the bowling alley on Seniors' Day with her own ball, bag and shoes just to bowl one game. This 45-minute workout burns approximately 90 calories.

Follow CasSandra:

Website: www.cassandrabelton.com
Facebook:
https://www.facebook.com/ArdnassacsUneekKreationsLLC
Instagram: https://www.instagram.com/Ardnassac_Kre8s

CHAPTER 5

Journey to Faith

by Danielle Scott

Sometimes, believing in the unknown of your future can become a scary thought. But, of course, we all have our lives planned out. So we think. By thirty, I wanted to be married with kids, live in a big, beautiful home, and be happy in my career. The funny thing about life is that it'll throw you an unexpected curve ball that can completely change the course of your life. Thankfully, I have always been one that doesn't mind taking a risk.

The Arts have always been a part of my life. At the age of three, I embraced Performing Arts through ballet dancing and started modeling later in high school. During the latter part of my teaching career in Detroit, Michigan, I was an Attendance Liaison for a public school called Hope Academy.

God always has a way of putting you in the right places to meet the people you need along your journey. I met a woman, beautiful inside and out, named Velda Hunter, and we became great friends. After one conversation, we clicked like sugar on candy. Velda is a well-known actress in the entertainment industry in Detroit. She was working on a web series named *Carter and Cody*. In the spring of 2017, the production company needed extras to film. Velda kindly thought of me and asked if I would like to come on set. I was so excited and responded quickly, yes, I will be there. I was blessed to work on two episodes of the *Carter and Cody* web series. That sparked my interest even more in becoming an actress.

Acting was always a thought to pursue, but I didn't because of fear. I wasn't the strongest student growing up. I actually struggled a lot in school. I was bullied, picked on, teased and wasn't the best reader. There were many challenges I had to face that hindered my ability to go forth into acting. I constantly thought about reading the scripts and if I would read well. The thought of it would give me anxiety. Therefore, acting became a thought hidden in my heart. Until Velda invited me on set. I started to think maybe this could be a possibility for me. However, the fear came up again, and I moved on with life.

At the top of 2018, after working in the field of education for eighteen years, I decided to make a career change. I resigned in March 2017. I lost my love for teaching; it became stressful when we had to teach to test the children and not for them to learn. It took the fun out of learning and educating the children. When I left teaching, I was hired by a digital marketing firm called White Glove. It was more money than teaching, and I got a chance to travel with the company.

Even though I was no longer working at Hope Academy, Velda and I remained friends. She invited me to her birthday celebration in January 2018. Since this was in January, cold wintery weather in Detroit, I wasn't sure if I would make her party. In addition, my new career in the corporate world had me traveling. I hadn't seen Velda in a while and wanted to support her. So I pressed my way and went to her birthday celebration. I was so glad that I did. The producer/director of the web series *Carter and Cody*, Melissa Talbot, was there. I was so excited to see her. As I sat there staring and contemplating whether I should say something to her and if she remembered me, I wondered all kinds of questions. Finally, I thought to myself, here's your chance, Danielle. You're getting older, and if you don't take a chance on yourself, you may have regrets. Also, you may never get this opportunity again.

Finally, after thirty minutes of having a full-blown conversation with myself in my head, I walked over to Melissa. "Hi Melissa, my name is Danielle. I was an extra on the *Carter and Cody* web series. Do you remember me?" Excitedly, she said, "Yes and hi, how are you doing?" I said I was well. Then out of nowhere, I said, "I really want to get into acting. I believe I'm ready, and it's time." I was so nervous; like, what did I just say? Melissa responded, "Great!" She was about to start production for a stage play called *Dear Future Husband*, and she would follow up with me. Of course, when people say that, you instantly think they're not going to. Melissa kept her word!

She reached out to me on social media and tagged the writer of the play in the message. I was so happy. I was finally going to overcome this fear that had haunted me for years. The audition date was set, and I was prepared to present my sixty-minute monologue. I was so nervous that if you had touched me, I would have fainted. Thankfully, the room was not filled with many casting directors; it was Melissa and her business partner Richard Bass. That eased some of my nervousness. They called me in, and my knees were shaking badly. They responded with a serious and intense look, "Whenever you are ready." I took a deep breath and performed the monologue. After I was finished, they said, "Thank you." They had more auditions and would let me know by email if I received the role. I was glad it was over so I could stop sweating and shaking.

But, it was not over because waiting for the email was next. Oh boy, I had to stay busy, so I would not worry about receiving the role. I decided to focus on the positive, no matter the outcome; I was so proud of myself for overcoming this fear. Stepping out there and taking a chance on myself. This was big for me. Within days, I received the email. I was scared to open it; my heart was beating so fast. Finally, I opened it. "Dear Danielle, we are pleased to offer you the role of Denise in the upcoming stage play *Dear Future Husband.*" I was at work when I received the news. I jumped for joy and ran down the hall to share with my coworkers, that knew I had an audition. They shared that moment of victory with me hugging and jumping up for joy in the middle of the hallway. Then I thought to myself, what a sense of humor God has; I want to be married, and He has me in a play called *Dear Future Husband.*

Life as I knew it changed for me that very moment I received the email. The Lord began to open doors for me in acting. I went full speed ahead, giving my all to acting, taking classes, and building my resume. One audition led to another audition, and by this time, the *Dear Future Husband* stage play was going to

Atlanta, Georgia, in March 2019. We ran the play back-to-back in March and May of 2018. By the end of the year, I was cast in three films and another play, *Unequally Yoked*, by playwright Vanessa Lynn. God had blessed my mind. I could not believe this was happening.

However, with all the excitement and the life I always hoped for came devastation. Even though I overcame this fear, a very dark cloud was still hanging over my head. I could smile in a room but feel lonely and empty inside. Yes, I am a woman of God, pray, love the Lord, all of that. Yet, I battled with some emotional and mental scars. Scars that laid deep in my soul. Some wounds you can't heal overnight. They take a little more tender loving care. A process to work through, talk through and feel through. I am grateful that God placed powerful women of God around me to always get the care I needed. However, this is an individual walk, and there are just some things that you have to work out on your own. I was in a new place in life but stuck in pain. I needed some deep soul healing.

That same year in 2018, my spiritual mother, Vera, was diagnosed with cancer. I could not believe that this was happening. I met Vera when I was twenty-six years old. She had been a spiritually sound woman in my life for years. I would often tell Vera thank you because she genuinely saved my life.

By the time 2019 arrived, Vera's health began to decline significantly. We were set to perform the play *Dear Future Husband* in March in Atlanta. While preparing for the road, I was also coming out of production with the play *Unequally Yoked*. I was right by Vera's bedside every chance I got between working full-time and play rehearsals.

In January, a few of the cast members and I went to Atlanta to promote the play for the show in March. I had been to Atlanta twice, once in January and back in March, for the actual performances. We were set to perform two shows on March 31, 2019. That morning of the play, we were all excited and getting ready. I laid in bed thinking of Vera and saying that I was going to see Vera as soon as I got back home. I could not wait to tell her about my experience in Atlanta. Within seconds of me saying that, my phone rang. Vera's sister Janice called to let me know Vera had transitioned. I dropped the phone and became numb. I remember walking through the hallways of the Airbnb, trying to find my friend and cast mate to share the news with her. When I reached her door, I cried uncontrollably in her arms. Vera was gone, and I still had to perform the play. How would I make it without her? She played such a vital role in the woman I had become. I knew Vera would want me to go forth in strength and handle the rest when I returned home. The play was a huge success, and I got through both shows.

When I returned home, God began dealing with me about moving out of my townhome. The townhome I lived in had bad plumbing problems that caused my basement to flood several times. In my mind, I thought I would find another apartment to live in, in Michigan. However, I really wanted to move out of Michigan. I was thinking of moving out west, like California. My lease was to be renewed in September of 2019, and realistically I just didn't have the time or finances to make such a big move. The place I lived in required a sixty-day notice, so, by faith, I submitted my notice to leave the premises in July 2019. I had this strong urge in my spirit that I had to move. I felt like if I didn't obey God, I would spiritually die in Detroit. So, I was procrastinating packing and looking for a place to live.

Detroit was the only place I had known all my life, born and raised. My birthplace had also brought me so much pain, and I wanted to leave. I struggled with that inner battle. My family reunion was coming up, and you'll never guess the city hosting it: Atlanta, GA. What were the odds of that—back in Atlanta a third time? I told my Mom I didn't want to go. I had been to Atlanta twice that year for the play and wasn't interested in going again. However, when God's plan supersedes yours, there is no way of getting around it. My mother kept asking and making the way so easy that I could not say no.

So there I was, back in Atlanta again. This time I could enjoy it because the other times were for acting. As I walked the streets of Atlanta, I saw things differently. I said to myself, Atlanta isn't so bad. It's actually lovely. That was just a thought because I wanted to be married, and surely my husband wasn't in Atlanta. There's too much going on here, I thought to myself.

When I returned home, I went back into production for the play *Dear Future Husband*. We were on our third round of performing the play because it had become the most talked about show. The show dates were close to the end of August. I still had not packed or looked for a place. My brother kept telling me, "Danielle, you have to begin packing. Once you start packing, the Lord will open the door for you." I knew the Lord was speaking through him because I was slothful in moving. I still didn't obey the Lord. I kept saying I'll get to it like I had a lot of time.

One day, my brother and I decided to go to the movies after visiting one of our family members. I wanted to stop at my home to change clothes before going. I told my brother to wait in the car while I went in and changed. Walking down the basement stairs, I stepped in water. I was thinking to myself, where did this water come from? I looked over the basement stairs, and it had flooded worse than ever. I began crying, running to the car to tell my brother what had happened. His words were, "Danielle, I told you weeks ago to start packing." It was as if God was saying it Himself. I had no choice but to get busy packing and cleaning. I lost a lot of items in the flood. I told myself as soon as the play was over, I would look for a place to live. However, I started cleaning and packing. I still was pushing it because my lease was up at the end of September, and the play was towards the end of August.

The play was over, and moving had my full attention. One evening, I was praying, seeking the Lord on where to move while cleaning. As I was cleaning the hall closet upstairs, I heard the Lord so clearly, and loudly say the word in my ear, "Atlanta." I took a step back, like, did I just hear the Lord say Atlanta? I responded back to him, "Atlanta, Lord?" I was scratching my head, feeling puzzled. I repeated it, "Atlanta, Lord? You know what's in Atlanta, and Lord, I want a husband. I really want to be married, and I know Atlanta has a mixture of many things." I heard the Lord say, "Are you putting me in a box?" I repented and said, "Lord forgive me." I never want to put God in a box as if he doesn't know His plan for my life. After that, yes, Lord was my answer. I will go.

My cousin had been living in Atlanta for about three years, so I called him to ask about housing and what cities I could live in that would be safe. He was so excited that I was thinking of moving to Atlanta. Which made me even more excited. He offered me to live with him because he had enough space and could also use the help. At first, I thought living with someone could be hard at times. But then, I thought I could really use the break, be able to save money, and it would be easier to find a place to live since I didn't know much about the Atlanta area. So, I decided to become my cousin's roommate. The next task was asking my boss if I could move to Atlanta and work remotely.

After Labor Day weekend, I returned back to work and spoke with my supervisor the moment I arrived. I was so nervous. What calmed me was knowing that if it was God's will for me to move, it was already done. Thankfully, my supervisor was aware of the flooding I had to endure and that I was looking to move. Her response was, "I will have to speak to the CEO of the company to get their approval." It took about two days for her to respond. In the meantime, I continued packing and cleaning. I even set my date to move to Atlanta on October 5, 2019.

Finally, the wait was over; she called me into her office once the workday was over to discuss their decision. She said, "Do you want the bad news or good news first?" I said, "Just give it to me." She said, "Well, the good news is they gave you the approval to move and work remotely." The bad news was I would have more eyes on me since I wouldn't have supervision. I was like that's it, piece of cake, I got this. We were so excited, jumping up for joy at the news I had just received. I called my cousin in Atlanta to tell him my good news and that I would be moving there on October 5th.

I couldn't believe the miracle that had just occurred. Then, finally, my heart's desire was answered. I was moving out of Detroit, Michigan. With only about twenty-two days left before I had to move out of my townhouse, I had no time to waste. I didn't want to take any of my furniture because I wanted a fresh start when I moved to Atlanta. I didn't want anything to remind me of Detroit. All things new is what I believed God for.

The Lord told me to invite my family and friends for a weekend moving sale. The sale took place on a Saturday and Sunday. My family and friends came over in droves to purchase items. I sold everything that I needed and wanted to sell. There were just a few items I kept and placed in storage. The Lord blessed me so well that I had more than enough money to begin my new journey. I had an array of mixed emotions. One thing was for sure, I knew I couldn't move to Atlanta with a dark cloud still hovering over my life. It was imperative that I was free from that dark cloud because I did not want to bring the old into the new. God being who He is, always sets you up.

My next-door neighbor Keisha was a hairstylist and did a beautiful job braiding hair. So I thought I would get my hair braided. She was battling something spiritually and ended up being my answer to prayer. Keisha began to share with me something that happened to her as a child that remained a scar in her adult life. She said she had to return to the little girl she was at the age and time it happened. Keisha found a picture of herself when the trauma occurred and spoke to the image as if she was that age again. She had no idea what she had done for me. Keisha had poured into my life in a way I had never heard of before.

I went home and pondered our conversation, in awe of how God ordered my steps. By this time, my furniture was gone, but I kept the couch from my basement to sleep on. I didn't sell the couch because it had water damage from the flood in the basement.

The Lord woke me up early the following day. I woke up talking to Him, still thinking and thanking Him for what happened at Keisha's house. I told the Lord that all my younger pictures were packed away. I wanted to take myself through the same experience as Keisha. Suddenly, the Lord said you have a photo on the table. I responded Lord, I sure do. I had a picture on the table I hadn't packed because my mom had found it. I went to the table. It was a photo taken when I was three years old at the daycare I went to called Sleepy Hollow. When I saw that picture, I knew I needed to return to that age because something had happened to me. I remember bits and pieces from the daycare but knew something occurred at that age that I barely remembered. I began to talk to the picture as if I was talking to three-year-old Danielle. I looked at the picture, weeping and crying, saying *I promise you that Adult Danielle will take better care of you.* I made a promise to myself that as an adult, my future was going to be so much better. I felt so many weights lifted off my shoulders. That was a start, but I knew there was more to do to lift the cloud.

I was asked to minister the word of God the Sunday before moving out of my home. The last room I had to pack and clean was the basement. I didn't have much to do because I had done a lot after the flood. But there was a particular area under the basement stairs of old boxes I had to go through. Since I had to preach the word of God on Sunday, I wanted to have it done so I could focus on the message, not knowing that God would use that as a setup for the word I would preach. I began to clean up and noticed a pattern I had created. I kept old pictures and things I should have thrown away years ago. There was a common theme in the photos I took of such sadness. Writing in journals and scrapbooks about just wanting to be happy. I had old wedding pictures of when I was married. Stuff I had kept and never took the time to let go of. All that stuff of the past: hurt, pain, discouragement, and setbacks had traveled with me from house to house. What did I do?

I placed all the painful memories in the basement and let them sit there for years. That was my revelation. It was my breakthrough of the dark heavy cloud that followed me for years. I cried as I sat on the stairs throwing things away I should have gotten rid of a long time ago. God sealed the deal when I ministered to the women at God's Way Deliverance Church that Sunday. I poured out to those women in a way I never did before. I knew it was mostly for me. I prayed that I would not move to Atlanta with this dark cloud. And I did not. I felt it lift off of me as I poured into those ladies. Sharing with them my story of healing and deliverance. I was finally free from it all. Really free mentally and emotionally. The gratefulness I felt once the service was over was profound. God honored my prayer.

I moved out of my home and stayed with my parents for a week before moving to Atlanta. Everything you can think of happened that week to try to prevent me from moving. The only thing that kept me on track with moving was my friend driving with me had already purchased her plane ticket to return home. If not, I would have probably changed the moving date five times.

October 5, 2019, had arrived, and I woke up early in the morning to leave. We were on the road at 4:00 a.m. to arrive in Atlanta by late afternoon. As we were driving, I could not believe I was about to start a new life in a new city alone. Such bravery to start life all over again at forty-three years old. Was I nervous? Absolutely, the unknown of will I make it and be successful played a massive role in my nervousness. God did not tell me why I was to go to Atlanta. He did not lay out the blueprint of what I was to do. All He said was just go, and I obeyed Him.

It's now 2022, and I have been living in Atlanta for three years. Wow, how time flies. I can honestly say that living in Atlanta has been good for me and good to me. I love living here. I have such unexplainable peace and happiness here that I have never felt. I don't just wake up to assist and go through the motions of life anymore. I live in Georgia. I create moments to live life to the fullest. Has it been cake and ice cream? No, it has not. With every new beginning and obeying the plan of God will bring the storms of life. I have experienced the wilderness, the pandemic, being laid off from my job, and losing friendships, which is too much to dive into. I'll save that for a later date and another book.

Meanwhile, through the ups of downs, God has still been faithful. One of my prayers to God is, Lord, you brought me here, and I know you'll keep me here. He's done just that. The doors that God has opened since I lived here have been amazing. I have been in three stage plays, five films, one television sitcom, one voiceover, one improv comedy show, and a photo shoot for a women's clothing line, and I have my own talk show called *Catching Conversations.* Just recently, one of the films I played a lead role in, *The Last Rose,* aired on a nationwide cable channel, Aspire TV. God is so awesome; the film appeared on Aspire TV four times in October, once in November and once in December 2022. I began writing my first book when I moved here. The title is called *The Foundation in My Basement.* I share more profound things about my life experiences and how I overcame them. So much healing came into my life once I began to write.

My journey to faith in obeying the plan of God has been one of a kind. We all have our stories and experience life in different ways. I challenge you today to take a chance on yourself. Whatever it is that you desire to achieve, now is the time. There is no fear that you cannot conquer. The faith within you can overcome any obstacle that tries to stand in your way. You are fearfully and wonderfully made. Keep in mind that we live in this world, so we will face some challenges. However, learn through those challenges and grow through and prosper from them. Accept them as they come knowing that God will always fight every battle for you. If you never take a chance on yourself, you'll never experience what's on the other side.

Start writing down what you would like to accomplish and what you need to complete, and set a date to have it done. Focus on what makes sense and is reasonable, and you can begin immediately. There is room for you in the industry you desire to go into. I thought I was too old to start acting. When, for me, it was the right timing. I am mature enough now to handle the coldness this entertainment industry can bring. Jeremiah 29:11 says, "For I know the thoughts that I think toward you, saith the Lord, thoughts of peace, and not of evil, to give you an expected end." Do not rob yourself of another day. People are waiting on you to share your gift with the world. Lastly, if God did all that for me in just three short years, imagine what He will do in the next three years. We haven't seen anything yet!

ABOUT THE AUTHOR

Danielle Scott's goal is to one day contribute to the field of Business Administration through the gift of entrepreneurship. Born and raised in Detroit, Michigan, Danielle is the middle child of three siblings. She moved to the beautiful state of Georgia in 2019, where she resides. Danielle currently works in the automotive field. In addition, she is a trained, certified Life Coach. Her gift is to empower women to become better versions of themselves. She believes we must first believe in ourselves to pave the future that only we can achieve.

Danielle graduated from Western Michigan University and was awarded a Bachelor of Arts. The Performing Arts have always been a part of Danielle's life. However, she is ready to make a career change that will produce happiness and success and make her dreams a reality by pursuing an acting career. Danielle was cast in four hit stage plays and in several independent films. In addition, she completed an MBA at the University of Phoenix Master of Business graduate program. Danielle is a very determined and dedicated woman who has a goal in mind and seeks the opportunity to one day make a contribution to society through the marvelous work of business administration, life coaching and acting.

Facebook: Danielle Scott
Website: www.daniellescott.net
IG:_imdanielle_nicole

CHAPTER 6

Beauty for My Ashes

by Brittany Henton-Henry

It was a beautiful, sunny July day. It was weather perfect for a stroll in the park, a bike ride or even a picnic. The clouds looked as fluffy as the cotton candy I loved as a child at the county fair. The skies were a perfect shade of serene blue. However, I wasn't outside enjoying the weather; I was looking out the window from my hospital bed in a cold, sterile room, anxiously waiting for the doctor to tell me the results of my lab work.

Just two weeks prior to this moment, my life was completely normal. I had a job that I enjoyed, an extensive social network, a loving family and perfect, vibrant health. Then, in the blink of an eye, my pristine life had come to a screeching halt.

I had come down with a persistent fever that would not break. I had no other typical symptoms that often accompany a fever: a runny nose, cough, and aches. But I felt chills. Down to my bones, chills. Finally, one night my fever got to 102 degrees, and I began feeling delirious. I was rushed to the hospital, treated with IV fluids and given a fever reducer. The doctors suspected it was a virus, prescribed antiviral medication, gave me a note for my job, and sent me home that night.

Two weeks passed, and the fever had not broken. Then, one particular night I felt like I'd been hit by an eighteen-wheeler truck, with the wind knocked out of me. Glancing at the clock, I saw it was nearly midnight, and I was restless. I tossed and turned, my body violently rocking with aches, my fever scorching at 104 degrees.

The room was slowly spinning as if I were on a merry-go-round. My heart raced, and my palms were sweaty. Black flashes kept going across my eyes, and every breath was a struggle. I gasped for air as I staggered to the bathroom to get dressed because I knew something was terribly wrong and that I needed to go to the hospital.

When I looked at myself in the bathroom mirror, I heard the enemy whisper, "This is the end. Say your goodbyes to your parents. You are going to die." I was spiraling down and felt like I was going to collapse on the cold bathroom floor. The room was no longer slowly spinning; now, it was out of control. I felt myself blacking out, so I called for my parents. My dad came, carried me from the bathroom and gently laid me on the couch while my mom called 911.

A thunderous knock came pounding at the door. Two paramedics rushed in and took my temperature, reading a startling 104.8 degrees. They told my parents that a persistent fever at such a high level could cause a seizure. I was carried out on a stretcher and raced to the hospital, and my parents frantically followed behind. I could see the reflection of the ambulance emergency lights through the back window. The wailing sirens rang in my ears, and it seemed like the longest ride of my life.

When I got to the hospital, my fever was still extremely high, and my pulse was 180 beats per minute at rest. I was given a fever reducer and another medicine to help slow my heart rate. Unlike my first ER visit, the doctors seemed very alarmed this time. They asked my parents a slew of questions about my medical history and found that I had a clean bill of health. The doctors concluded that I did not have a virus, but they could not pinpoint the cause of my fever. I was admitted for an overnight stay and watched as the doctors frantically hooked me up to multiple IVs. The nurses would wake me up throughout the night to draw blood like clockwork. It wasn't long before my arm was black and blue from being pricked and prodded so many times.

Many days and tests later, the doctors were still without a diagnosis. Then, one day, I heard a gentle knock on my door. The doctor came in with a stern demeanor and sadness in his eyes. He took a deep breath, and my parents and I braced ourselves. I had a feeling that this news wouldn't be positive.

The suspense was unbearable. My heart was racing, and my stomach knotted up like a pretzel. The room went silent in anticipation. The only sounds you could hear were the light humming from the AC and the beeps from the monitors that thumped with my racing heartbeat.

My dad broke the silence. "So, doctor, what is causing her symptoms?" he asked.

The doctor looked at me and revealed that I had an aggressive and dangerous form of lupus. He explained that the illness was a chronic autoimmune disease that causes your immune system to turn on itself and begin attacking healthy cells and organs. He informed me that chemotherapy treatment is often used to limit organ damage. "There is no cure for it, and you will need to be on medication for the rest of your life," he said. Additionally, the lab work showed that my kidney function was declining and needed supervision. The diagnosis rang like a death sentence. I was confused and in denial.

I was only twenty-five years old. Healthy. No one in my family had lupus. I heard about this disease for the first time in my life that day. I have always prioritized my health by exercising, taking vitamins and supplements and eating reasonably clean.

My parents stood by my bedside and held my hands. I could see them trying to conceal their worry, but I saw their watery eyes. I took a deep breath and, with tears in my eyes, prayed the following prayer: *God, show me natural remedies to overcome this. Lord, please, heal me so I can share my testimony, and many people will be encouraged and blessed by it. In Jesus's name, amen."*

With a proud look, my dad said, "You will get through this, Britty. You know we are here for you always. God will keep you. He will not leave you or forsake you." My mom nodded in agreement.

After a week's stay, I was finally discharged from the hospital. I was ecstatic. However, the joy I had quickly dissipated when I got home and reality set in. Every morning I was in excruciating, debilitating, tormenting pain unlike anything I had ever experienced. My headache was so severe that it radiated and locked my neck, limiting its mobility. My joints were inflamed and throbbing. Recently retired from his job, my dad would come in, bring me food and rub anointing oil on my neck.

I rarely had an appetite, although I had to eat to take the prescribed pills. Crackers, ginger ale, and water seemed the only items I could tolerate without feeling nauseous.

Before heading to work, my mom would help me out of bed to shower. Normal, everyday activities were laborious. I ached with every step, and the short walk from my bedroom to the bathroom felt like 500 miles. My mom would have to place a stool in the shower for me. Standing was unbearable. "If I could bear this pain for you, I would do it in a heartbeat," my mom said. But she couldn't. Even if she could, I would never want her, or anyone, to experience this kind of torture. Questions would race through my head in the shower as the warm water merged with my tears: God, why me? What did I do to deserve this? I felt like a victim. Helpless. *This sucks. I just miss my old life.*

The glimpses I had of my old life were swiftly fading into mere distant memories. This was my new normal.

Nothing on TV excited me. I went from having a busy social life to lying in bed in agonizing pain daily. My movement was limited to only the shower and the bed. To pass the time, I found myself reading the lupus pamphlet the doctor gave me and doing internet searches to learn more about the disease. The more I learned, the worse I felt. Although my parents would come and pray for me daily, the prayers weren't reaching me. Friends and family also prayed and gave words of encouragement to no avail. I felt alone. No one truly understood the level of physical and emotional trauma that I was experiencing.

Sensing my withdrawal, my mom suggested I join a local on-line support group for people diagnosed with lupus. I excitedly joined the group, hoping to find encouragement. However, to my dismay, the group was filled with such posts:

"Who else woke up in debilitating pain?"

"The doctor just added a new medication, and the side effects have been horrible."

"Having lupus sucks."

"A family member of mine just died from lupus; sending love to all suffering from this wicked disease."

"The doctor just told me I need to go on dialysis because lupus ruined my kidneys."

The posts exacerbated my worries, dragging me deeper into despair. I craved edification, and that led me back to my roots, the church.

I grew up in church. However, at the time, I was in between churches. I remembered my cousin's invitation to visit her church in times past and asked my parents to take me. My steroid medication had kicked in, providing minimal yet sufficient relief. I pushed through the aches with my parents' help, determined to get to my cousin's church.

On the day we went, the ushers greeted us with smiles. I remained seated during praise and worship because of my pain level, but I observed the exclamation around me. For a moment, my pain faded into the background. I cried out to God in pure yet roaring worship, needing Him desperately.

The pastor preached about the importance of changing our confessions, praying and declaring the Word of God. He said we had to change our mindset and uproot the negative thoughts from the Enemy. We must fiercely believe what we are standing in faith for, sight unseen. I knew this message was for me. He even stated that you must believe you are already healed and see yourself healed. The pastor's passion was contagious. Hope seeped into my heart.

God spoke loudly during the pastor's message and gave me specific instructions. He told me to do the following: go to the store and buy foam poster boards. Look up every scripture about healing in the Bible and write them down. Then, post the boards around my room and speak the scriptures over myself daily.

I realized that with the adverse medical reports and deep research into the disease, my mind was saturated with negativity. The doctors' reports replayed in my mind like a never-ending song. My mind became a playground for the Enemy, and he had a field day with me, but I was ready to turn the tide.

After church, I went to the store and purchased the items. Still in pain, I did as God directed and was immediately revitalized. The scriptures were planted in my heart as truth.

I ripped the lupus pamphlet into tiny pieces, throwing it away. This began a symbolic rejection of all of the negative reports. Instead, I believed a new report—the report of the Lord.

I shifted from researching lupus statistics and cases to googling testimonials of God's healing of the disease. I created an environment for my faith to thrive and understood that I was diagnosed with lupus, but it did not belong to me. It was not my portion. Healing was.

The pain endured, but I felt encouraged and lifted from hopelessness. I was going to church every week and feeding my spirit. As a result, my fellowship with God deepened, and I heard His voice clearer than ever. My flesh felt weak, but my spirit held ox-like strength. God was no longer merely the God of my parents. It was now personal: He was *my* God, and *my* God told me that He was going to fully heal me.

I stepped out on faith and recommitted to exercising. One morning, I went to the park and walked half a mile. As I was walking, I prayed and declared scriptures. My strength increased, and I progressed to walking a full mile and then two, reclaiming my mobility. For the first time in a while, I felt great and experienced minimal pain.

My parents noticed the significant changes in me, and it strengthened their faith. Finally, it seemed like normalcy was on the horizon.

I had a follow-up appointment with the specialist that had given me the diagnosis. I went into the office for blood work with God-backed confidence.

A few days later, the doctor's office called and urged me to come in immediately. On the way there, fear began creeping in, but I recited my healing scriptures.

When my dad and I arrived, I was surprised to learn that my blood pressure and temperature were elevated. So naturally, this made me nervous, and I began fidgeting.

My dad touched my knee and said, "Relax, Sweetheart. Just breathe. It is well." His calm voice assured me. "By His Stripes, you are healed. " I repeated those words.

The doctor informed me that the attack on my kidneys had worsened, their function decreasing from 64 percent to 34 percent. I was referred to a kidney specialist. I also had a low-grade fever, signifying my current medication's ineffectiveness, so I was prescribed yet another drug.

This one was deemed excellent; patients who took this drug outlived those who didn't. However, the doctor cautioned that long-term use could cause vision deterioration, so an optometrist would need to monitor my eyes. Great, another doctor!

"You will need to be on medication for the rest of your life, or your disease will get progressively worse, leading to organ failure and even death." That's what the doctor told me, but I did not agree. So I didn't let his words marinate in my spirit. Instead, I bound the words up and replaced them with scripture: "I shall not die but live and declare works of the Lord."

Unfortunately, it didn't stop there. Because of my high blood pressure reading, I was now required to see a cardiologist and follow up with my primary doctor biweekly. A cardiologist? Decreased kidney function? My dad and I looked at each other in disbelief. My mind was flooded with thoughts as I left the office. *But God, I was obedient. I wrote the scriptures. I decreed them over myself daily as you instructed. You said you would heal me. So why are the results worse?* I felt myself beginning to spiral. However, I refused to return to that dismal place, devoid of joy and peace.

I went home and did the only thing that would calm my fear—I studied and confessed the Word of God. I candidly asked God to keep me encouraged, regardless of what I saw and heard, but a subsequent appointment confirmed that my kidneys were in further decline. I needed a kidney biopsy for further investigation and was prescribed *more* medication to stabilize my kidney function. I was already taking a mountain of pills every day.

My cardiologist did an EKG on me to see how well my heart was functioning, and the results came back abnormal. My blood pressure reading was 210/112, so high that the doctor informed me that my pressure was at a stroke level and was putting dangerous stress on my heart and kidneys. To my dismay, he immediately prescribed two different blood pressure medications and directed me to wear a heart monitor for a week for more research. After a week of wearing the monitor, the results came back normal. My heart was not damaged. With a sigh of relief, I rejoiced over this praise report. I needed to hear positive news!

I was spending more time going to numerous doctors' appointments than I did at home. Eventually, I'd quit my once-loved job because I could not return anytime soon.

Defeat crept in. Once anchored with healing scriptures, my thoughts were marred with fear and disappointment. With each appointment, the miracle I believed in seemed intangible. Even after revamping my diet, taking supplements and changing my lifestyle, the results worsened despite my decrees, fasting, and faith.

A few weeks later, I woke up and noticed a cluster of red bumps on the side of my stomach. At first, because of the pattern, I thought it may have been caused by a spider bite. However, because they itched, I wrote them off as mosquito bites. The next day, more and more clusters appeared on my stomach. After the second day, the clusters spread more and became blisters. By day three, I was in excruciating pain. My parents took me to the doctor's office, and I was diagnosed with shingles resulting from the steroids that suppressed my immune system.

The shingles spread from my stomach and wrapped around my back. The constant throbbing of the blisters felt like someone was waving a flaming torch against my skin. The blisters left ugly, darkened scars throughout my body. My appetite was extremely low, and I was frail, my weight dropping to ninety-nine pounds, a size I hadn't seen since middle school. Though discouraged by yet again another blow, I held on to my confessions.

The shingles caused me to miss a few appointments with my kidney specialist. When I finally went in, I feared the worst and tried to neutralize my thoughts with scripture. Nevertheless, my eyes widened with nervous anticipation when the doctor walked in with my lab results.

I was diagnosed with stage 4 kidney disease, with stage 5 in sight. She informed me that my kidneys were failing and that I would need dialysis training and a kidney donor for a transplant soon. *The devil is a liar. That's not my portion. No weapon formed against me shall prosper,* I thought to myself.

In a wave of faith, I boldly declined to participate in dialysis classes, and I told her that I would not need to be added to the transplant list. She was very unhappy with my decision and strongly cautioned me against it, offering me a dialysis training pamphlet in lieu of my attending the class. Again, I politely declined and told her I wouldn't need dialysis.

Despite standing in faith for my healing, that night, I felt discouraged. With back-to-back blows, it began to feel like I was the brunt of a malicious joke. When I thought I was taking a step forward, the blows thrust me backwards. As a result, there were no confessions or declarations that night. Instead, I sat in the dark silence and cried myself to sleep.

The next morning, my discouragement mellowed, and I woke up renewed, continuing to stand on the Word of God. Weeping surely endured for a night, but joy truly came in the morning. Revitalized, I held onto every word God promised me and stayed committed to my exercise and dietary changes.

Suddenly, my blood pressure dropped so low that I had to rush to the doctor. The drop in pressure pleased the doctor, and I was taken off one of the blood pressure medications and received a lower dose of the second. It was a turning point, a light at the end of a long tunnel. Additionally, my steroid prescription was decreased. I finally saw the fruit of my prayers.

The good news continued at the following appointment with my kidney specialist. To my doctor's surprise and amazement, my kidney function had significantly improved. If that wasn't enough, she gave me a big smile and said, "I'm pleased to tell you that your kidney disease is now in remission."

She said in remission, but I heard *HEALED*. Just as God promised. No dialysis needed. No going on the transplant list. I was elated and grinned like a six-year-old on their first trip to Disney World.

"What have you been doing exactly?" the doctor asked. I told her I had been praying, exercising, and making specific dietary changes. She told me she would start recommending the regimen to her other patients.

"God is good," I said. She nodded in agreement and said, "Yes, He is. This is truly a miracle." So that night, my family and I celebrated the miraculous news!

I was taken off every lupus medication that I had to take since my diagnosis and was weaned off of the medicine for my kidney function. At that point, my kidney function had nearly doubled! The doctor's visits were moved to a few times a year, and normalcy returned to my life. Finally, I had my health back!!

I was so excited! God brought me out with a powerful testimony of healing and unshakeable faith. I told everyone I knew about

God's healing power. I praised God and thanked Him for keeping me! I prayed for and encouraged those who were sick, and people were encouraged by my testimony.

Most importantly, this period cultivated a deep, meaningful relationship with God like never before. I realized that my journey was so much bigger than me. God used the situation for His glory and to accomplish His purposes for change and impact. Every tear I cried over the last few months was overshadowed by this unspeakable joy.

With a clean bill of health, I was ready to officially re-enter the workforce and get back to building my career. I interviewed for a position I wanted at the bank and was hired! I felt like a champion boxer that was nearly K.O.'d but came back in the last round to take home the victory. Full of gratitude; things could not get better!

I was seven months into my new job and loved it. My boss and my co-workers were amazing. I felt fully back on my feet. Then, one day when my manager released the new work schedule for the week, I saw that I had a Saturday off, which was rare. I was delighted!

That weekend, the weather was picture-perfect. I was driving, listening to music, and celebrating my day off. I was heading to get my hair braided at a friend's house. Following the GPS, I arrived at her complex, got into the correct lane and prepared to make a left turn. Suddenly, out of nowhere, a large Jeep came flying up the hill from the opposite direction. The driver was distracted and hit me head-on as I waited in the turning lane. The airbag deployed. I remember taking off my seatbelt and crawling out of my car. Covered in blood, I collapsed into a pool of my own blood. It looked like a murder scene. Thankfully, a kind onlooker stopped and called 911. I found my phone and managed to call my dad.

Because of the shock from the accident and the adrenalin racing through my body, I did not feel the pain until I was in the ambulance. Then, I remember my head throbbing and the paramedics wrapping my right hand because a bone was sticking out of it. Apparently, I had bitten down to the bone of my hand while placing it in front of my face to shield myself from the airbag's impact.

When I got to the hospital, I learned the full extent of my injuries. My dominant hand was broken, and many bones were utterly shattered. I lost my front tooth. I had fractured bones in my face and at the back of my skull. Additionally, I had a large lip laceration on my mouth and fractured my nose and the roof of my mouth. I didn't recognize myself. My face and lips were about three times their usual size.

When I got to the hospital's trauma department, my blood pressure was 198/112. The doctors were concerned that the airbag's impact may have caused bleeding in my brain and significant damage, so they quickly rushed me to get an MRI & CT scan. As I was waiting to be taken into the examination room, the Enemy tried to whisper myriad lies to me. I kept saying Jehovah Rapha, my healer, repeatedly and quoting as many healing scriptures as possible. At that moment, all I could do was whisper Jesus over and over again and thank God in advance that my scans would come back normal. My faith muscle memory from the lupus journey kicked right back in.

The MRI/CT scan revealed no damage to the brain, no fluids or bleeding on the brain. To God be the glory! That accident could have easily killed me, but God shielded me.

The doctors said the fractures in my face were lined up perfectly, so I didn't need pins or surgery on my face and would heal over time. Likewise, the laceration on my lip over time healed beautifully. I began healing so rapidly and made improvements in such a short time that someone said I heal like Wolverine (*X-Men*), but that was nothing but Jesus's supernatural healing.

I was surrounded by the best of family and friends, who showered me with so much unconditional love. Through the accident, I indeed saw my then-boyfriend's heart toward me. He stood beside me during my recovery and at my lowest points. He came to my house faithfully, prayed with me and tenderly cleaned my lip laceration. Those moments were forever etched in my brain. His unwavering support was a Godsend.

During my months away from work while going through physical therapy, surgery and recovery, my boyfriend and I studied together for our real estate test, and both got our licenses. We always wanted to delve into real estate, and now I had the time to learn. We extended our education into real estate investing. Months later, we purchased our first property and successfully flipped it.

Within that period, my boyfriend and I both heard God clearly tell us to leave our jobs. Though we were extremely nervous about the unknown, we were obedient and delved into real estate full-time together. We knew we had the backing of the Lord. Before long, we made more financially as real estate investors than we had ever made at our salaried jobs combined. We went on to flip multiple properties and acquired both long-term and short-term rental properties. God breathed on the business, and it prospered beyond what we imagined. God directed our paths and gave us the wisdom needed to succeed. He got all the glory!

Six months later, we were married and had an intimate ceremony. My father, an ordained preacher, officiated my wedding. It was pure bliss.

The life I was now living was such a contrast from the previous years of trial after trial. It now felt like blessing after blessing. I would often reflect and would be overwhelmed with gratitude. The Lord had not just restored me, but He renovated me. My whole life improved. Both incidents I experienced were God's loving course correction for me. I was exactly where I needed to be and who I needed to be.

I now saw myself for who God said I was: powerful, fearfully and wonderfully made, here for a purpose and here to share my story for the glory of God. All the pieces started to line up like a puzzle, and everything made sense. What the Enemy meant for evil to kill me, God turned it all in my favor. He restored everything stolen from me during those years and gave me *DOUBLE*! He is a God of recompense! God made everything beautiful in its time and gave me beauty for my ashes. He turned my mourning into dancing and gave me a garment of praise to replace my once-heavy spirit. For that, I am forever grateful. Though each test did not always feel good walking through it, God used it for His glory. My story had to happen exactly how it did for God to mold me into the woman that He created me to be. Tried in the fire but came out like gold. I was a new creature.

Here is this girl doctors told would be on lupus medication for the rest of her life, now living free of all of them. The girl, the Enemy, tried to take out and kill multiple times, is still alive and well. Not just surviving but thriving by the grace of God. The faith roller coaster changed me. Transformed me. God truly walked with me through the fire, but I got out not smelling like smoke. I share my testimony, and people are shocked, often telling me that I don't look like what I've been through.

Out of every brokenness, I learned to find beauty. I'm confident that God really does work all things together for my good because I love Him and am called according to His purpose. No part of my story has been wasted. On the contrary, God has used and will continue to use my story to get the glory out of it. This, indeed, was my rebirth.

ABOUT THE AUTHOR

Brittany-Ann Henton-Henry is a successful Georgia-born Jamaican American real estate investor, licensed real estate agent and a twenty-first-century entrepreneur. Brittany is the co-founder of four thriving real estate enterprises. Each venture speaks to different facets of the real estate industry, including real estate development, vacation rentals, property staging and supporting clients in searching for and acquiring their forever homes. Brittany is a proud magna cum laude graduate of Georgia State University, where she obtained a degree in marketing. In addition, she is a certified life coach, real estate educator and real estate consultant.

Brittany is a visionary businesswoman who has taught classes and workshops and provided one-on-one training to help educate clients on how to strategically achieve their real estate dreams and goals. In September 2021, Brittany was recognized as her branch's top-selling realtor for Maximum One Realty. In the same year, she was honored by the metro Atlanta-based Caribbean Association of Georgia, Inc., for her contributions to Georgia business as a Caribbean American and burgeoning business leader.

Brittany is a proud woman of faith whose faith in Christ informs her entrepreneurial and humanitarian endeavors. She and her husband, Kareem Henry, have supported local and international initiatives through Hosea Feed the Hungry and Homeless, The Caribbean Association of Georgia's Youth Symposium Scholarship Program, Books for Africa, and various other humanitarian organizations.

Brittany is also an incredibly gifted interior designer and furniture refinishing artisan who can easily transform dated spaces and pieces into premium contemporary looks.

Check out some of her work and get to know more about Brittany by following her on Instagram @thatssobrit.

CHAPTER 7

Fractured but Not Broken

by Tiney Ray, PhD, DNP, FNP-BC

Introduction

Where do I start? I had a dysfunctional childhood, was a high school dropout, and was a teen mom. Why am I here? If my life sucks and it will be so hard, why even bother? I have carried these thoughts, questions, and beliefs for many years. I don't even stand a chance. My mother hated me, and my dad did not have good luck choosing nice women. You know what I mean. They were friendly in front of him, but I was given the stank eye once he left the room.

I knew my dad loved me but is it possible for a father to love his children too much? I can say no unequivocally, but it was a different story back then. Being held accountable for the sins of my mother and for sins I hadn't even committed yet was a heavy burden to bear. I heard repeatedly, "you are no good," "you will not amount to nothing," "you are worthless," and "you will never be good enough."

That was in stark contrast to my father, who would tell me the opposite, "you are a queen," "you are special," and "you are brilliant and powerful."

What should a young mind believe? But unfortunately, the most impactful were the negative things back then because they came from women who looked just like me.

The sad thing is I fulfilled their perception of me, and I was that kid that ran away, dropped out of school in the Ninth Grade, became pregnant at seventeen, and was homeless and on welfare. Now what?

The Beginning

In the 80s, my role models were my pregnant high school dropout girls, who were just as clueless as I was. I admired these girls. To me, they had it all. They had children, lived on their own, and received money and food stamps from the government. What was not to love?

They had it all. The state paid for their housing, childcare, food, and everything. At the time, I wanted to get away from my parents and be on my own, so I believed the only way to have "freedom" was to get pregnant, so I could get all the things my friends were getting. So, I got pregnant. Wow, did I get a rude awakening.

Listen, you will have to understand my point of view. My mom was not your average mother. I was privileged to see how poor choices due to untreated mental illness can destroy the people that love and depend on you. On the other hand, I could see God's grace for His imperfect people. But let's be honest, all I could see was the horror and the embarrassment of being the child of this flawed woman. I was a kid with limited ability to see it from anyone's point of view.

This may sound crazy to you, but I will say it anyway. All my struggles, I mean the ones inflicted on me unwillingly and those I caused due to my poor choices, were lessons that shaped and molded me into the full-grown adult woman I am today. I know what you are thinking. Yeah, she's crazy. How can you find any lessons in being used, abused, and on the route of poor decisions? I am here to tell you this was the route I needed to take to see God's glory. Keep in mind that this is my journey and perspective, and you can look at your struggles as you see fit.

I grew up thinking my mom never loved me. She would belittle me in public as well as in private. Growing up, I thought I would never be good enough to do much of anything. What a way to start life. Observing how the woman in my life treated her friends, coworkers, and family left me thinking it was every woman for herself. Take no crap from anyone, and if you have to stomp on a few heads, oh well, that is just part of life. I also thought it was normal for women not to get along. That was my only explanation for why she did not like me. Makes sense, doesn't it?

What makes a woman a woman? Is it the way she moves, or is it nurturing intuition? One of the things I always longed for was that female encouragement, words of wisdom, and guidance. I was able to get that through my pretend role model Oprah Winfrey. I remember when her show debuted. I was in awe of a Black woman who was kind, intelligent, and curious. She had everyday people on her show, but the most memorable were the vulnerable women who displayed their issues on national television. Oprah respected them by not judging and berating them for viewership. She was the kindest woman I knew then and taught me so much. But was this how a woman was supposed to be? Act? I was so conflicted. What I saw and heard on television from 4:00 to 5:00 p.m. was nothing I was experiencing in my real life.

So, needless to say, my mother and I never saw eye to eye. I dropped out of school in the Ninth Grade. Even when she found out I was pregnant at age seventeen, that did not change our relationship. I was just another knocked-up girl with no future. I remember hiding my pregnancy up until my fourth month. Then, my prenatal clinic called the house, and my mother answered the phone. After that call, she called me every name in the book, which led to one good thing. Usually, as a punishment for not following her rules, she would take my bed away, and I had to sleep on the floor. Well, let me tell you, after the call, she gave me the box spring to sleep on. Wow, she was starting to loosen up. As I got along in my pregnancy, getting on and off the floor was difficult, but at least I had something to sleep on. That was a blessing.

Another thing I picked up from "the people who love me" is that when you mess up, there may not be anyone by your side. My father and I were close until he discovered that "his baby girl" was pregnant. He expressed his disappointment and refused to speak to me during my entire pregnancy. It wasn't until I was officially homeless and until after I had my baby (to be exact, when he was six weeks old).

My entire pregnancy was stressful, and to tell you the truth, I had no business being pregnant because I was totally clueless. Between being verbally and mentally abused by my mother and the father of my child threatening to kill me and physically abusing me every day, I wondered if I would ever survive. Also, in the late 80s and 90s, many teenage girls my age were murdered by their boyfriends. So, I genuinely believed I would never live past the age of thirty. I was clueless about how to take care of myself, but it was too late; my son was coming. But to be honest, I had a hard time looking forward to the future.

Being homeless with a kid was not my idea of making it. In my mind, I thought the state would set me up with an apartment right away. But the joke was on me. I bounced around from shelter to shelter with my baby and garbage bags of my personal belongings in tow. I was going nowhere fast.

I remember a family member dropping me off at the social service center at 11:00 p.m. one night with my six-week-old baby and four garbage bags of clothes. I remember it like it was yesterday. I was terrified because I had no idea what would happen to my baby and me. Sleeping in a chair (with one eye open) with a baby lying on my chest was brutal to me, physically and mentally. And this homeless period lasted for five years.

My life changed one day while I was living in a motel shelter. I was feeding my son and heard a knock at the door. I didn't open the door, but I did ask who it was. It was the hotel pimp, and he told me to open the door. That was enough to get my head on straight. The motel offered a GED tutor; I remember being the first and only person who took advantage of the offer, and I was there every day. After that, I knew I had to get an education to have legal choices in making a life for my son and me. Luckily, I passed the GED, so my next step was to go to college. This pivotal milestone was the first thing in my life that gave me hope for the future.

No one can ever tell me that having my son was a mistake. At the time, my concern was for him and wanting better for him. I did not correlate my struggles as a test for something more significant in my future; all I had to do was "hold on" and keep going. I did that and stayed the course. I proudly say I am not a scared teenage girl. I pushed so hard that I earned two doctorate degrees. How is that for perseverance? I wish I could tell you the struggle was over, but it was just beginning. With all that I have gone through, I still struggle. For a long time, I wanted to prove myself to others, to show that I was not a screw-up, mistake, or burden.

So, the new thing I tell myself is, "I'll show them." You may be asking, "show who?" Hey, I know I am not the only one who does this. It is a known fact from reputable behavioral scientists that trauma affects how our brain functions on various levels, from how we make decisions, think, feel, and act to subconscious responses to our surroundings (1,2,3). So, when I have these feelings of inadequacy, I will generally engage in something that will take my mind away from these thoughts. That may be disassociation or detaching from my body, feeling as though the world around me is unreal, going to school, learning something new, or starting a new project. This may not sound bad to you, but for me, it is distressing. Distressing because I ignore the feelings and emotions behind these behaviors, and doing these activities brings up a lot of stress. This long-term stress has had some physical implications for me, such as hypertension, insomnia, anxiety, and probably some other things I have not yet discovered. The point is that the coping mechanisms I have used in the past that saved my and my son's life worked well back then, but they are irrelevant and useless now. So, what do I do?

Our brain is an amazing organ. Did you know there is a part of the brain that stores every piece of information and experience that you may not recall when asked, but if something happens, an emotional trigger can be almost anything? It is often based on an event from our past we try our best not to repeat. It could be a tone of voice, a personal characteristic, a misplaced joke, or a blunder that would typically be brushed aside. For example, any sudden hand movement from a person with an agitated tone of voice puts me in an uncomfortable place where I go back in time to when I was being hit with a golf club while being called names. I am in my fifth decade of life, and it does not matter if my thoughts at that time are logically correct or overly emotional if my body is having a physiological reaction to it.

The saying time heals all wounds is false. The passage of time does not make it go away. This is incorrect. Time does not heal all wounds because emotional wounds are in the part of the brain where there is no sense of time. Our emotions are not logical; if they were, we would all be able to figure our stuff out, and there would be no problems.

My Lyght Bulb Moment(s)

For years, I have blamed others for my life adversities, giving all my power away to anything outside myself. I finally realized that giving away my control robs me of my mental strength, which is exhausting. I am not the only one who gives people and circumstances power over me. However, I can identify those areas of my life where I gave away my strength, which is the first step in taking it back.

My imagination helped me, and I was really good at dissociating myself from the chaos. But I can channel it in a new way. I do not ignore my feelings or the current reality, but I choose to see the glass half full. Everything is about choice. I have the option to pick myself up and leave a situation. That was not the choice I had when I was a minor; I had to stay and bear it. I have the option to make different choices than my parents and others around me. No, I don't think I am better than anyone, but it is best to break this cycle of useless thinking, which harms my well-being and keeps me further from my purpose. My purpose is to help others, and I will not be able to do that with outdated thinking.

I read and follow most of the brilliant minds of Bishop T.D. Jakes, Dr. Michael Bernard Beckwith, Oprah, and Dr. Myles Munroe, just to name a few. When listening to their teachings, the overall message is to stay in my lane. So many things are happening in this world. It is easy to be overwhelmed by the grief of listening to and watching all the bad stuff we are distracted by, unable to see the good. My response is to stop, breathe and acknowledge these things are happening, but the focus is on what is in my control. I cannot control what people are saying or not saying about me or what they are thinking and not thinking.

Does it still bother me? Heck yeah, at times, but the difference is it does not paralyze me, and I keep focused on my purpose so I can move forward.

Forgiveness

I love and respect the unique perspective of all thought leaders on forgiveness. They all say, "forgiveness is for you and not the other person." I understand that, but it is hard when you are amid emotions brought on by someone screwing you over. I would repeat, "forgiveness is for me," but saying that was not helpful. If it helps you, let me know. How can I make this concept of forgiveness work for me?

Years later, it clicked I had to start by forgiving myself. I had to forgive myself for my negative thoughts, bad decisions, indecisiveness, and for allowing others to make choices for me. I had to forgive myself for calling myself bad names and causing physical and mental harm to myself. I had to forgive myself for thinking I was less than others and for the feeling that I didn't have the right to be here. God makes no mistakes. If you are here, there is a purpose for your life.

Relationships

Healthy relationships are critical to our health and well-being. On the other hand, the health risks from being alone or isolated put us at risk for chronic physical and mental illness. The key word is "healthy." Not all relationships are good, and knowing the difference is equally important. The circles of relationships can help us better understand how we relate to people, what our interactions should look like and where to invest our resources with priority. I make every effort not to make my new relationships pay for the past ones. Every long-term or temporary relationship is here to teach us something. But most importantly, we are at the core.

The closest and most intimate connection we have is with ourselves. It is no one's job to help me feel complete and vice versa. That is my job. I do not look for anyone to complete me; that is not their job. Instead, I look for relationships that complement my completeness. But this takes work on my part. Are my mind and body prepared to take me to my life's purpose? What I mean by this is that I am putting things in my body that do not serve me and are harming me, such as excessive alcohol use, eating foods that are not nutritious to my body, etc. How do I fill my own cup? What are my self-care practices?

Don't Follow the Crowd

Following after others is never a good idea. My experiences with following the crowd never worked out well for me. This herding behavior is when most people do what others do just to fit in and be accepted at the cost of their dignity and self-awareness. Yes, we are social beings, but if the reason for not making our own decisions is because of fear of making the wrong decision or that others may not like the decision, it will not give you the outcome you may have expected. I can tell you that all the decisions I made that did not turn out well were because of this. And I was the one to blame because, deep down, I knew better than that.

I relied on the herd to guide me and provide the answers to things so I would not have to make the decision because what if the decision was wrong? What if I follow the herd and the decision they make for me is wrong? Who is to blame? The answer is I will be to blame. God has given us free will and the freedom to make wise choices in our daily lives. These choices we make each day can either help us mature in our faith or gradually destroy the foundation of our beliefs. I will be wrong by giving away my power to others.

Everyone is on their own journey. I had to learn that the specific desires of my heart come from God. These desires and visions may differ from mine, but that is okay. These visions and desires don't belong to anyone else. They are mine!

I view the freedom of choice as a gift and a privilege. This freedom gives us dignity, agency, freedom, and respect, so why would I give that away? You may say, "yeah, but what if the decision is wrong? There are a few things I do when making important decisions. The first thing I do is identify habits that require little thought on my part because they're automatic. Then I give myself time (with no one else's input) to know if these automatic responses are serving me. For example, I know that jaywalking is illegal (in most states, if not all); listen, I am from New York, and this is what we do because we have places to go. And I have jaywalked many times without incident.

One day, a friend of mine and I were running late for a conference we were attending, and we did what we always did and ran across the bustling Manhattan street. Well, that was the day my friend was hit by a taxi. She was okay and got right up, but the cab driver got out of his car and started to yell at us. Of course, our feelings were hurt, but we were in the wrong when I thought about it. Now, when I think about it, I stop and think about the pros and cons of not following pedestrian laws.

Another thing I do is when I'm faced with a decision, I frame the issue differently, think of the pros and cons, and then leave it alone. I don't dwell on the subject. The answer will come to me. There have been times when I have been pressured to decide quickly, and when I did that, it never, ever, ever turned out well for me. I blamed the person or people for pushing me to make a decision when I wasn't ready, but in reality, the blame was all on me.

I always look for the lesson in my decisions, whether they turn out well or not. I don't dwell on my mistakes for too long as this is not good for my mental ability, and rehashing my missteps over and over again isn't good for my mental health, and it keeps me further away from the job I am supposed to be doing. Making it a daily habit to consider the mental shortcuts that lead to bad decisions is work, but it is necessary. Another thing I do is not make any decisions due to emotions because emotions change frequently. Talking to yourself like a trusted friend takes some feelings out of the equation. It will help me gain some distance from the decision and be more objective.

Ultimately, it's your life, and you are responsible for all your success and failure. So, before following the herd, remember that life doesn't allow you to complain later if anything goes wrong with your decision. In the face of uncertainty, everyone makes bad choices, and if you have higher emotional intelligence than others, you will think more about all the possible negative consequences. However, unless and until your decisions involve other people's lives, you should never be fearful of the plans you make and the actions you take.

The Gift of Giving

I enjoy helping others. I have learned over the years that I feel much better when helping others. This spiritual gift of giving strengthens my belief in recognizing God's blessings and responding to them by generously, sacrificially, and cheerfully giving my time, talent, and treasure without thinking of return. There is also a science to kindness. The warm feeling of well-being washes over me when I've done something kind. This warm feeling releases hormones that contribute to your mood and overall well-being. Many mental health professionals incorporate this into their treatment plans.

When God gives you a message, you better listen. The first time may be subtle, but the next one may not be so comfortable. COVID was a blessing for me. I was running myself into the ground, and my breaking point was in October 2020 when I contracted COVID. It stopped me in my tracks, and I had no choice but to surrender and listen. The fatigue and brain fog made it, so I had to drop activities that were not serving His purpose. It forced me to take care of myself and reflect on my journey and goals.

Fear was my problem, but fear is not an excuse. I was fearful of success, disapproval, and rejection. I have come to realize that my fear is of someone saying "yes" because I did not believe in my ability to help others. So, the logical thing to do is to overcompensate for perfection with other things. The problem is that this fake success just strengthens the overcompensation of fear, which is not helpful because it increases fear. This puts a distance between what I want to give the world and who I really am. The further away I am from it, the better I thought I would be. This is an essential concept because if you are really good at hitting the wrong target, you have not made any progress. You are just getting good at hitting the wrong target. And what happens is our brains perceive the illusion of success. This fear-based solution had to stop, so I had to build courage and act despite fear instead of fighting it. I proved to myself that I would not die or wither away when I made the leap. I had to trust myself. If not, I would be my own worst enemy. Fear can empower some situations, but I will not let it take over my life. This is a non-negotiable requirement of my growth.

Thank You

On April 15, 2022, at 7:11 a.m., my stepfather called to tell me that my mother's condition was worsening, but he still hoped she would pull through. Being in the nursing profession for thirty years, I knew she would not survive this, and she needed to be in hospice, but my stepfather was in charge, and I respected whatever decision he made. I then wrote my mother a letter that I knew I would not read to her in person because I was in Georgia, and she was in New York. Therefore, I typed up this letter for myself to read out loud for closure and to say goodbye. This is the first time I am sharing this with anyone.

Dear Mommy,

I want to start off by saying thank you so much. Even though we have not had the best relationship growing up, I forgive you. I've always forgiven you. My goal was to seek to understand why things happened. That's probably what makes me seem so curious. I understand that God put us here on this earth for a purpose. We all have a purpose in this life. We are not here to have a good time, collect stuff, and be gallivanting around the world, but there is a job that we are on this earth to do.

Even though you have struggled for so many years with mental and physical ailments, God had a purpose for you. I believe that you were here to show us a different way. If it weren't for you, I don't think I would be the person I am today. Your purpose was to touch the lives around you, and even though much of the touching was not all good, I now understand that all experiences can be viewed as teachable moments, whether good or bad. It's all up to us how we look at it.

I look at all of those bad experiences as blessings because I'm able to better understand you as a woman and human being. That has led me to the profession I am in now. I continue to ask questions, listen and learn so that I can help others. Rest in peace. If God decides to take you now, I believe your job is done. God makes no mistakes.

Love you, Tiney

My mother died on May 1, 2022. She was two months shy of her sixty-ninth birthday.

Conclusion

My journey has not ended. As long as God gives me breath, it allows me the opportunity to change my mind about an idea and learn something. When someone asks me how I am doing or how my day is, I always respond with everything I am grateful for. I was told the other day that I sound like an old woman. I chuckled and answered that if you had been where I have been, you would be grateful for just waking up in your right mind. When I think about those who did not wake up this morning or have lost one of their senses, etc., I am glad I was spared another day to do His will. Enough is enough! I vowed never to let hurt and shame run me out of my home. People will never be able to see how hard I fought to survive. I am a survivor, and there's is no shame in that.

My Prayer

God, give me strength, resilience, and clarity, and cover me. I know you did not make any mistakes when you made me. Time and peace belong to me. I know you are watching over me. I know my grind and hustle are for a purpose; I am not perfect. I may have fractured pieces that started in childhood, but I am not broken. The best way to kill a dream, my self-esteem, and so on is when it is in seed form. And you have covered me. You protect me from my enemies, seen and unseen, including myself, not knowing which of my fractured pieces you will use as my testimony. I am living proof that you are a God of mercy and grace. I will honor you all the days of my life. In Jesus' name. Amen and Amen.

ABOUT THE AUTHOR

Dr. Tiney (pronounced tīnē) is a Certified Life Coach based in Georgia. She earned her Bachelor's and Master's degree from the College of New Rochelle in New York and her Doctorate in Nursing and Ph.D. in Public Health and Community Education from Walden University. Her holistic approach brings clarity, direction, and positive support to her clients. Dr. Tiney helps clients live their best life by filling the gap between where they are now and where they want to be. As a result, clients will reach their highest goals and dreams by identifying where growth is desired, setting goals and objectives, and holding accountability.

Are you going through a stage in your life where you feel lost, confused, or conflicted? Do you feel disconnected from the people around you, friends, coworkers, or even yourself? Are you feeling a lack of motivation or lack an understanding of your true purpose? Do you yearn for a romantic partner or the perfect job? Or do you just want to upgrade your life to the next level? Dr. Tiney is trained to help people find themselves, find direction, and true happiness in all aspects of their lives. We all have a light within us. You are already born with the qualities you need to get everything you want! Dr. Tiney helps her clients reach each milestone one at a time, with the ultimate goal of satisfaction and success. You can follow Dr. Tiney on multiple social media platforms at https://linktr.ee/LyghtBulbMoments.

References

Duffee, J., Szilagyi, M., Forkey, H., & Kelly, E. T. (2021). Trauma-informed care in child health systems. *American Academy of Pediatrics, 148*(2). DOI: 10.1542/peds.2021-052579

McNally, P., Irvine, M., Taggart, L., Shevlin, M., & Keesler, J. (2022). Exploring the knowledge base of trauma and trauma-informed care of staff working in community residential accommodation for adults with an intellectual disability. *Journal of Applied Research in Intellectual Disabilities, 35*(5). 1162-1173. DOI: https://doi.org/10.1111/jar.13002

Racine, N. Killam, T, & Madigan, S. (2019). Trauma-informed care as a universal precaution beyond the adverse childhood experiences questionnaires. *JAMA Pediatrics 174*(1), 5-6. DOI: 10.1001/jamapediatrics.2019.3866

Made in the USA
Columbia, SC
07 February 2023

11262088R00080